The Fundamentals of Austrian Economics

The Fundamentals of Austrian Economics

by
Thomas C. Taylor
Wake Forest University

Published in association with

The Carl Menger Society

 Adam Smith Institute

Acknowledgement
The Adam Smith Institute and the
Carl Menger Society wish to
thank the Cato Institute of
Washington, D.C., for their kind
permission to produce this
British edition of *The Fundamentals
of Austrian Economics.*

Second edition
Published by The Adam Smith Institute
ISBN: 0-906517-15-X

First published in 1980 by the Cato Institute, ISBN: 0-932790-27-5

Published by The Adam Smith Institute
in association with the Carl Menger Society

Printed by FotoDirect, Brighton, England

CONTENTS

Do the barriers to entry to of a market, due to its inhibiting competition, defeat the labour theory of value? Does the L.T. of V. attempt to explain barriers to entry?

L.T. of value

Price = costs of production

Costs of production = price of direct + accumulated labour involved in making the product

Lack of accurate information is surely a huge barrier to entry

Marxism + austrian economics are based on the idea that once you get the economics right - in line with their perfected theories - everything else will fall into place. They completely ignore the social side + its relevance for creating

1. INTRODUCTION

The history of economic thought, like that of other disciplines, reveals a mixture of systems of thought that have been separated into particular schools of ideas. This method of categorizing the ideas of different thinkers concentrates on the likenesses of certain groups at the expense of overshadowing their differences. The French Physiocrats who rose to prominence during the second half of the eighteenth century represent the first modern school of economic thought. Classical economic thought, Marxism, and socialism subsequently followed. During the latter part of the nineteenth century there emerged in western Europe two clashing schools of economic thought: the German Historical school and the Austrian school. The German Historical school sought to discover economic truth through the study of economic history. In 1883 their empirical methodology became the target of the early Austrians, who maintained that economic knowledge arises from theoretical analysis and not from the study of history. For more than two decades, the *Methodenstreit*, or controversy over methods, persisted.

This book is an attempt to explain the essential ideas of the Austrian school, which began with Carl Menger, professor of political economy at the University of Vienna from 1873 to 1903. In 1871 in his *Principles of Economics (Grundsatze der Volkswirtschaftslehre)*, Menger produced a theory of value that was to resolve the question that had so long perplexed the great classical economists. This theory was the subjective theory of value based on the principle of marginal utility.[1] It dispelled the classical notion that the value of a thing is an objective measure intrinsic in the good itself. Economic goods were now seen to be valued subjectively in terms of the satisfaction that the user expects to derive from their incremental use. A more thorough treatment of the subjective theory of value, which was to become the foundation of the whole Austrian system, is presented in later sections. It remained for Menger's two great disciples, Friedrich von Wieser and Eugen von Böhm-Bawerk, to refine the subjective theory and to clarify its full ramifications in the areas of cost and capital and interest theory.

Wieser expanded on Menger's problem of imputation, which explained resource prices or costs as being derived from the expected prices of the consumers' goods that the resources were used to produce. The formation

---

[1]The history of economic thought now credits Menger, William Stanley Jevons, an English economist, and Leon Walras, a French economist, with having established independently the subjective theory of value at roughly the same time. See M. Blaug, *Economic Theory in Retrospect* (Homewood: Richard D. Irwin, Inc., 1962), pp. 272–73.

of value was thus shown to be a circular process, and the concept of costs, a gap in Menger's theory, was tied into the subjective theory of value. Wieser's "law of cost" or doctrine of alternative costs held that the costs of producing a product reflect the competing offers of other producers for the resources used in production; costs are merely payments made necessary in order to attract resources away from their next most remunerative utilization.

Böhm-Bawerk's great contribution was his theory of capital and interest. He emphasized the significance of time in the economic process and defined capital as the produced factors of production. The crucial idea in his analysis was that "roundabout" means of production enable humans to increase their productivity, both in terms of increased quantities of goods producible without equipment and tools and in terms of goods producible only through capital goods. The period of waiting resulting from the use of indirect processes provided the basis for his explanation of the phenomenon of interest. He argued that people value present goods more highly than future goods with similar characteristics, other things being equal. This assumption contained the basis for justifying the margin between selling price and costs, the margin that went to the capitalists who supplied the funds for intermediate products or capital goods. Their return was an interest payment for the period of time during which their investments had been used and was not an exploitation of the workers, as Marx had contended. Thus the subjective theory of value was expanded to include the time-preference principle. Although the Austrian theory of capital was somewhat revised, Böhm-Bawerk's essential explanation of interest and the process of roundabout or indirect production has retained a dominant position in present-day Austrian theory.

Two important modern theorists in the Austrian school are Ludwig von Mises and Friedrich von Hayek. Mises received widespread attention from other economists in the 1920s with his challenge that socialism was totally impossible in a modern economy because of its lack of market prices, for him the indispensable means of rational resource allocation. Both Mises and Hayek have contributed significantly in molding the Austrian theory into an integrated whole. Their explanation of cyclical swings in business as resulting from uncontrolled credit expansion at the hands of government added another significant block to the Austrian structure. Hayek's focus on the problem of "knowledge in society" and the vital need for co-ordinating the actions of interacting market participants has provided insights of crucial importance to the study of economics. This book will draw substantially from the ideas of Hayek and Mises, along with those of two students of Mises, Israel Kirzner and Murray Rothbard, both of

[margin notes: Does this prove labour value theory wrong?]

[margin note: Argument against Marx's theory of surplus value & exploitation]

[margin note: Explanation of cyclical swings as a result of uncontrolled credit expansion at the hands of Government. Why?]

whom have made significant contributions to the elucidation and elaboration of the Austrian analysis.

Although the Austrian school is no longer distinguished from other schools in its acceptance of the subjective theory of value, marked characteristics remain inherent in the Austrian approach to economic analysis that set it apart from others. One such characteristic is its rigid methodological position. Reference has been made already to the *Methodenstreit* that Menger initiated in a book published in 1883.[2] Austrian economic analysis is carried out largely on the basis of theoretical, deductive reasoning; empiricism has little place in Austrian economic theory—thus their battle with the German Historical school. Economic phenomena, originating from a social environment, are deemed by the Austrians too complex and variable to permit the kind of experimental analysis that the physical scientists use. Accordingly, Austrian theory is opposed on methodological grounds to mathematics as a tool of economic analysis. Conceptual understanding, not quantitative relations, is seen as the only meaningful basis of economic science. Menger, the father of the Austrian school, insisted on and followed this qualitative orientation throughout his works, as did his successors.

The second important characteristic of Austrian theory is its methodological individualism. Austrians believe that economic phenomena are not the expression of some social force or hypostatized entity like "society." Rather, they are the result of the conduct of individuals engaged in economic activity. The total economic process cannot be understood, therefore, except by analyzing its basic elements, the actions of individuals.

The Austrian analysis uses as its data human nature and the realities of the human predicament. Individual human values and human actions, amidst limited means including perceived knowledge, are placed at the center of economic science. The factors of human error, the uncertainty of the future, and the inescapable passage of time must receive their due attention. This analytical approach cuts through the seeming complexities of an advanced market economy and provides a basic understanding of the economic process by examining *essential* market elements. Dispelled is any mystique surrounding the economy, market prices, business profits and losses, interest rates, inflation, and economic recessions and depressions. These phenomena are not inexplicable nor without cause, as will be shown in subsequent sections.

This book, as its title indicates, presents an overview of basic Austrian theory. Its focus is on the free market or capitalist economy. The seminal

---

[2]Now translated in English as *Problems of Economics and Sociology* (Urbana: University of Illinois Press, 1963).

4   works of the Austrian economists surely cannot be neglected for a deeper understanding of the topics herein discussed. These original works must be consulted, especially in order to obtain a thorough appreciation of the serious implications of governmental intervention into the market process, which is now rampant. Suggested readings for expanded understanding are provided at the end of each major section.

It is hoped that this book can serve as an effective introduction to the Austrian theory. (One can hardly avoid feeling some reluctance in using the term "Austrian economics" for fear of suggesting that it is perhaps something different from straightforward, sound economics.) The disarray of Keynesian economics, the bewildering artificiality of econometrics, the sad record of predictions by "professional" economists, unrealistic textbook models such as perfect competition and pure monopoly, persistent inflation *and* unemployment, and widespread politizations of economic interests have created a warranted distrust of all economic theory. Yet the Austrian analysis cannot be overlooked if a greater understanding of the market process and the effects of interferences with its operation is to be achieved. The book should prove useful as a supplement in a course in economic theory or a course in the history of economic thought at either the undergraduate or graduate level.

2. SOCIAL COOPERATION AND RESOURCE ALLOCATION

Calculations in Kind in a Primitive Economy

The task of economizing is as applicable to an isolated, self-sufficient person like Robinson Crusoe as it is to someone who lives in a society characterized by extensive division of labor and complex exchange transactions. Robinson Crusoe's task was to employ the means available to him in ways that he hoped would generate the greatest satisfaction. A process of deciding and choosing was essential to his welfare. Similarly, in modern society vast numbers of interacting individuals try to make the best use of all available means for want satisfaction. This economic problem exists whether the choices and decisions are largely left up to a centralized planning board, as envisioned in the theory of socialism, or whether such choices are made more or less freely on the part of individuals acting in a market economy.

Robinson Crusoe could effectively manage only a limited amount of resources and had to make comparatively few plans about directing their use. Because of the relative simplicity of his range of choice, he could make effective decisions without making any quantitative calculations about the possible results of different courses of action. His ability to assess or anticipate results likely would depend on the observation and intuitive grasp of the productive alternatives before him. Calculations in terms of physical output would suffice because his resources would not be highly diversified, and each resource type would lack, for him, a significant degree of versatility.

He would have access to some of the original factors of all production—land, including natural resources, and labor. However, because of his limited ability to produce goods in his isolated situation, these original factors could not be converted into a wide range of intermediate products such as machines and tools. He would be compelled to use the most rudimentary tools since he could neither acquire nor, given his situation, would he need the more intricate and sophisticated machines characteristic of a modern economy. Consequently, his decisions about how he should use the available resources to obtain consumption goods would not be so complicated as to necessitate some sort of objective profit and loss computation, even assuming the availability of something like money that could be used for computational purposes. The uses to which resources could be effectively put would be more or less determinable. The most versatile factor would be his own labor and ingenuity, which he would utilize in combination with natural resources to produce those products that he preferred and whose production was feasible.

His time and energy would be spent making basic tools, hunting for food, building a shelter, and producing clothing as well as resting. Given his particular situation and wants, he would not have to compile and compute data about the past or expected success of these uses of his time and energy and other factors of production. The limited nature of both his time and energy would prevent his exploiting the complete potential of his island's natural resources. His decisions would be based on a subjective calculus of profitability for each considered action; his alternatives would be so limited that he would be able to observe or anticipate the results of his undertakings in real terms in reaching such valuations. And since he would be producing for his own satisfaction, there would be no problem of his being unable to know which good among those producible should be chosen. His own scale of values would be the sole determinant.

A self-sufficient household could also manage its economic resources effectively without involved calculations of any sort, particularly if it had gradually developed a tradition of resource utilization. Whatever calculations of outcomes were necessary in these relatively primitive situations could be captured in terms of the various outputs, sometimes referred to as calculations in kind. Because of the absence of exchange relations there would be no medium of exchange and thus no common denominator for calculation purposes.

Calculations in Kind in an Advanced Economy

Over the centuries an alternative approach to economic self-sufficiency has evolved to deal with the problem of scarcity. This alternative is social cooperation, the basis of what is called society. Virtually all people have chosen society over self-sufficiency. The enormous increase in productivity resulting from specialization and the division of labor gradually undermined the process of self-sufficient provisioning. Yet despite the comparative abundance of products and services emanating from the process of social cooperation, the economic problem remains: Wants continue to exceed the means or resources for their attainment. The persistence of the problem of scarcity means that even in a modern, highly developed, and productive society decisions have to be made regarding how the various scarce resources should be directed to the satisfaction of the more urgently felt wants of the society's members.

These decisions are not as simple to make in an advanced society as they are in a primitive state of economic self-sufficiency. The resources cannot be as easily scrutinized for possible uses. The great enhancement of productivity arising from specialization and the division of labor considerably increases the flexibility of resource utilization. The fruits of social cooperation permit the devotion of a major portion of original resources, land and labor, to the direct production of what may be called producer's goods, or intermediate products, which ultimately will give rise to consumer's goods when combined with additional increments of land and labor. Here lies a crucial distinction between economic self-sufficiency and social cooperation: The complexity and intricacy of resource employment in a modern economy require far more complicated decisions than those that Robinson Crusoe had to make.

The increased complexity of economic decisions is partly attributable to the immense variety of consumer's goods and services that a high-level economy is capable of generating. Choices have to be made as to which ones should be produced and in what quantity; the larger the number of alternatives, the more difficult these decisions. However, decisions concerning ends are not the only vital decisions that must be made. As did Robinson Crusoe, people in society must make choices that relate resources to ends. How are the resources to be used? What makes this question hard to answer is that the economic resources in an advanced economy are extremely versatile and diversified. Their versatility can be traced to the wide range of uses to which they can be adapted as a result of advances in technology and productive skills, results that include the beneficial effects of the division of labor and specialization. And these numerous adaptations entail the conversion of original factors of production into a diversity of produced resources, thereby creating countless types of particular resources.

It is clear that with such an infinite array of steps that can be taken toward the production of finished products and services, the most economical or fruitful choices cannot be made simply by reviewing calculations in kind. The very abundance of resources makes it impossible rationally to assign and direct original factors of production to yield more refined means of production without some basis for comparison of the results. For example, iron can be used in the manufacture of locomotives, farm tractor equipment, textile spinning and weaving machinery, building frames, oil drilling equipment, and thousands of other items. Yet there is no way to compare the different results of these varied uses of iron without some means of translating them into common terms. And the problem is compounded when one remembers that for many uses other resources offer effective substitutes. Thus copper, tin, and aluminum can be used in place of iron or steel for certain items. The problem widens as the full range of alternatives is considered. Decisions concerning resource utilization would be a matter of immense confusion if calculations in kind were the only calculations. The allocation of scarce resources would be chaotic and seriously imprecise.

Once the shackles of self-sufficiency are removed and production for exchange is assumed, the epitome of which is a full-fledged market society, the need emerges for more precise calculations regarding the past and future outcome of resource uses. This requirement for keener calculations is met by the very factor that permits widespread exchanges to occur: money, the economy's medium of exchange. Monetary calculation provides an indispensable means by which a modern economy can translate the myriad of physically different resources and outputs into a common denominator. It is this monetary common denominator that provides the basis for an input-output calculus, a capitol-income calculus that is crucial to the allocation of scarce resources. This calculus is necessary because the scarcity of means requires the careful comparison of costs and benefits, of inflows and outflows in the production process.

It is generally agreed that in a modern economy calculations in kind are not the proper basis for resource allocation. A brief look at how certain leading advocates of socialism came to recognize the inadequacy of calculations in kind reveals that even the most enthusiastic opponents of the market economy now recognize the need for a common denominator for the purpose of rational resource allocation.

In 1920, Ludwig von Mises challenged the theory of socialism when he contended that socialism is unworkable in an advanced economy because of the inadequacies of calculations in kind.[1] He accused the socialist theorists of having ignored the critical task of resource allocation in a modern economy. They had assumed away this problem in their ecstatic belief that socialism is inevitable and thus naturally feasible. Not one eminent spokesman for the cause of socialism had bothered to explain just how rational decisions would be reached concerning the employment of scarce resources. Now they were forced to face the issue; faith in inexorable laws of history has no place in the realm of scientific discussion and inquiry. The socialist thinkers were challenged to resolve theoretically the problem of calculation.

Leading socialist theorists subsequently agreed that their theory was in need of elaboration on this point. They then began to explain how they believed that the process of allocation could be directed by central planners in the absence of competitively established market prices. What this explanation amounted to was the recognition that the planning authorities would require some method of calculating in common terms the ef-

[1] Ludwig von Mises, "Economic Calculation in the Socialist Commonwealth," paper republished in English in *Collectivist Economic Planning*, ed. F. A. Hayek (London: G. Routledge & Sons, Ltd., 1935), pp. 87–130.

fects of alternative economic actions.[2] They agreed that Mises was right in pointing out that they had failed to confront this matter in all of their previous works. They had been convinced that calculations in kind are insufficient in the management of a modern economy. Their replies largely culminated in the contention that the central planning authorities could establish prices through trial and error, guided by the existence of surpluses and shortages for each particular good. And these prices, stated in terms of the economy's medium of exchange, would serve as beacons in the task of resource allocation. Shortages called for upward adjustments in the prices of those items; surpluses signaled for price reductions. These price adjustments would lead to proper production adjustments—price increases would induce supply increases while price decreases would effect supply decreases—so that eventually equilibrating prices would be set, thereby removing various shortages and surpluses in both intermediate and finished goods. Resources would be employed rationally through the monetary guides issued by the central pricing and planning authorities. The socialist position now is that a socialist economy is not doomed to calculations in kind, and that, thanks to Mises, they had been spurred to demonstrate this point.[3]

The Problem of Coordination and Knowledge

The overriding difference between self-sufficient production and production on the basis of social cooperation is that only under the latter arrangement are people able to realize the overwhelming benefits of specialization and the division of labor. In addition, while a self-sufficient producer generates goods solely for his own satisfaction, an arrangement of social cooperation necessarily means that producers create products to satisfy other people. Virtually every person in a modern economy devotes his skills and energies to a highly specialized activity that provides a product or service to be used by someone else. We would all be in a sad state if each of us were suddenly compelled to produce only for himself.

[2]Fred M. Taylor, "The Guidance of Production in a Socialist State," *American Economic Review*, 19, no. 1 (March 1929): 1–8; also Oskar Lange, "On the Economic Theory of Socialism," *Review of Economic Studies*, IV, nos. 1 and 2 (October 1936): 53–71 and (February 1937): 123–42.

[3]Austrian theory nonetheless remains steadfast in its contention that economic calculation is impossible in a purely socialist society. Without actual market prices, edicts by central authorities become abysmally inept attempts to simulate market forces and are to no avail. See Ludwig von Mises, *Human Action: A Treatise on Economics* (Chicago: Henry Regnery Company, 1966), pp. 698–715. The fact that socialist societies today are able to utilize price information emanating from market societies must not be overlooked. Socialist decisions concerning resource allocations do not arise from within a purely and isolated socialist environment.

The reliance on the elements of specialization and division of labor worsens the problem of efficient resource allocation because it makes necessary some means of unifying or coordinating the separate plans and efforts of many actors. Underlying the problem of the division of labor, then, is the problem of what Hayek calls the "division of knowledge," which is "the really central problem of economics as a social science." Hayek has stated the central question as follows:

> How can the combination of fragments of knowledge existing in different minds bring about results which, if they were to be brought about deliberately, would require a knowledge on the part of the directing mind which no single person can possess? To show that in this sense the spontaneous actions of individuals will, under conditions which we can define, bring about a distribution of resources which can be understood as if it were made according to a single plan, although nobody has planned it, seems to me indeed an answer to the problem which has sometimes been metaphorically described as that of the "social mind."[4]

The seriousness of this problem of knowledge must not be underrated. Clearly a system of division of labor harbors the potential for chaos and confusion. If it is to work, there must be some means of synchronizing individual decisions and actions throughout the economy. For example, if the majority wants more timber to be used for the production of houses than for the production of paper products, then signals must be effectively communicated to induce this shift in resource usage. Otherwise a scarce resource will not be employed in the most desirable way; it will be employed for the satisfaction of less urgently felt human wants.

Yet the conventional model of so-called perfect competition, with its assumption of perfect knowledge, completely avoids treatment of the task of synchronizing decisions. The model assumes that knowledge concerning technology, tastes, etc., is given, and all individual plans are imagined as meshing consistently with one another. Knowledge is depicted as data similar to the facts used in the physical sciences. But this view of knowledge misconstrues the nature of knowledge in the social sciences. The knowledge that underlies human decisions and actions is grossly imperfect simply because a significant part of the "knowledge" in the mind of each individual consists of suppositions about the future decisions and actions of other individuals. These suppositions are subjective perceptions that are devoid of the certainty possessed by the facts used in the physical sciences.

And since a person's decisions and actions are likely to be modified as he gains additional experience of both external objective facts and other peo-

[4]F. A. Hayek, "Economics and Knowledge," *Individualism and Economic Order* (Chicago: University of Chicago Press, 1948), p. 54.

ple's decisions and actions, the notion that all separate plans and actions will eventually interlock and that the result will be a static, long-run equilibrium is totally unrealistic. By assuming perfect knowledge, the model fails to focus on the problem of the "division of knowledge." The model is a useful analytical construct in assisting the theorist's understanding of the logical result of an atomistic economic process in which unforeseeable changes were to disappear. But it is a construct that must be used carefully if the element of uncertainty is not to be erroneously omitted from the study of the real world.

Thus the task of rational resource allocation is not a simple matter of utilizing "given perfect knowledge" in the process of making economic decisions and actions. The knowledge that exists is "given" only in innumerable, scattered pieces and not in one single mind. Each individual has unique information regarding his particular circumstances of time and place, and others benefit from the actions taken by each individual because of his being particularly informed about his limited situation. However, because his particular information relates only to his limited situation, he may use his knowledge in a manner that is inconsistent with the plans of others. Social cooperation requires some method that will enable that part of each person's particular knowledge that is relevant to the plans of others to be disseminated as widely as possible. And this method must provide for the continuous dissemination of knowledge in the midst of relentless change. For as Hayek states, " . . . economic problems arise always and only in consequence of change. As long as things continue as before, or at least as they were expected to, there arise no new problems requiring a decision, no need to form a new plan."[5]

The coordination problem is inextricably connected to the fact that all data relevant to economic action is never simply *given*, as conventional price theory, dwelling upon the conditions of equilibrium, would have you believe. Market forces, the culmination of decisions by market participants—the consumers, entrepreneur-producers, and resource owners—are continuously effecting change in the market. What should be examined is not a static condition of equilibrium but the dynamic nature of the market *process*, striving unceasingly toward equilibrium. Decisions are made without perfect knowledge, which means the underlying data, far from being a *given* for all to use, are elusive and tenuous and available only by discovery and perception. Thus the market process is in essence a continuum of trial and error as new perceptions on the part of participants result in changes in plans and actions.

The driving forces in the market process are the producer-entrepreneurs who see profit opportunities arising from potential im-

[5]Hayek, "The Use of Knowledge in Society," Ibid., p. 82.

provements in market activities. The process of the market is ongoing because of the relentless search for profit and the resultant alterations in the market effected by competitive producer-entrepreneurs. While other market participants are more or less passive, unaware of or perhaps uninterested in profit-related opportunities, entrepreneur-producers search out and exploit profit potentials. The data they detect and act upon may be erroneous, and the subsequent realization of errors, manifested in monetary losses, provokes further alterations in the market. Once the condition of imperfect knowledge is introduced, price theory and the picture drawn of the market are vastly changed from that of orthodox discussion. The role of entrepreneurial profits and losses will be explored in greater depth in a later section.[6]

Suggested Readings

Hayek, F. A., ed. *Collectivist Economic Planning*, Clifton, N.J.: Kelley, 1975.

Hayek, F. A. *The Counter-Revolution of Science: Studies on the Abuse of Reason.* New York: Free Press, 1952.

———. *Individualism and Economic Order*. Chicago: The University of Chicago Press, 1948. Particularly the essays "Economics and Knowledge," "The Facts of the Social Sciences," and "The Use of Knowledge in Society."

Kirzner, I. M. *Market Theory and the Price System.* New York: Van Nostrand, 1963, pp. 33–44.

Mises, L. von. *Human Action: A Treatise on Economics.* 3rd rev. ed. Chicago: Regnery, 1966, pp. 143–76 and 698–710.

[6]For a penetrating analysis of the market process and its corollary, competitive entrepreneurial activity, see Israel M. Kirzner, *Competition and Entrepreneurship* (Chicago: University of Chicago Press, 1973).

The Role of the Price System

It has been shown that the essence of social cooperation is specialization and the division of both labor and knowledge. This fact has two significant implications for the purposes of this study. The first is that social cooperation results in the production of such a wide range of intermediate and final products that calculations in kind will not allocate scarce resources effectively. A common denominator is indispensable. The second is that the concomitance of decentralized decision-making and social cooperation requires a means of coordinating individual plans that are based upon imperfect knowledge and information. These two requirements are fulfilled simultaneously through the price system of the market economy. Detailed treatment of the workings of the price system will be postponed until later. At this point it will be sufficient to discuss the price system in general terms in order to demonstrate its dual function as a means of economic calculation and as a means of coordinative communication. Actually, as will be shown, these two functions are really of a piece; that is, they relate to the same problem of resource allocation under an arrangement of social cooperation and a system of market prices.

Economic Calculation vs. Technological Calculation

Economic calculation is not a technological problem. Technology can establish quantitatively the causal relations between a particular set of external things that can be used in various combinations to produce a particular result. The nature of technological calculation is that $6a + 4b + 3c + \ldots x_n$ will likely create the result $8p$. But technology cannot say whether the resulting $8p$ is the most desirable use of those particular quantities of resources a, b, c, etc., as compared with their possible alternative uses as means to the production of other ends. By the same token, technology is not able to say whether that particular formula for the production of $8p$ is the preferable one when $8p$ is also producible by means of other formulae or combinations of different resources. Mises has illustrated the problem as follows:

> The art of engineering can establish how a bridge must be built in order to span a river at a given point and to carry definite loads. But it cannot answer the question whether or not the construction of such a bridge would withdraw material factors of production and labor from an employment in which they could satisfy needs more urgently felt. It cannot tell whether or not the bridge should be built at all, where it should be built, what capacity for bearing burdens it should

have, and which of the many possibilities for its construction should be chosen.[1]

Max Weber made the same point in the following statement:

> The question of what, in comparative terms, is the cost of the use of the various possible technical means for a single technical end depends in the last analysis on their potential usefulness as a means to other ends.[2]

Technological calculations can only be calculations in kind. They are not sufficient for human decisions and actions because they are devoid of any preferential quality. The ivory-tower theorist may be right in claiming that an excellent tunnel can be built of platinum. But monetary calculation makes the issue an economic one, and the practical engineer is thereby discouraged from embarking upon such a scheme as long as platinum has uses deemed more important than the construction of tunnels. Technology is neutral to human valuation; it has nothing to say about the subjective use-value of the various objective uses for resources. As Mises has said, "It ignores the economic problem: to employ the available means in such a way that no want more urgently felt should remain unsatisfied because the means suitable for its attainment were employed—wasted—for the attainment of a want less urgently felt."[3]

Subjectivity of Value

The task of resource allocation is to satisfy urgently felt human wants, and therefore resources must be devoted to their most important employments. Yet the question must be raised as to how these most important wants or usages are to be determined. It would appear that some means of measuring the value of things is necessary to make these determinations, but this is not the case. There is no such thing as a measuring unit of value, and this fact means that measuring the value of a thing is impossible. Value is a subjective phenomenon that eludes cardinal quantification. A thing's value is in the mind of the person who is doing the valuing, and this process of evaluating is not a matter of measurement. Because valuation is always a matter of individual preference, ordinal numbers are the only type of numerical treatment that can be accorded the problem of valuation. This is the subjective theory of value which did not enter economic science until Menger, Jevons, and Walras introduced it in their analysis around 1871. Until that time, economists had searched for a source of value for all goods as if value were intrinsic in each good.

[1]Ludwig von Mises, *Human Action* (Chicago: Henry Regnery Company, 1966), p. 208.
[2]Max Weber, *The Theory of Social and Economic Organization* (New York: Oxford University Press, 1947), p. 162.
[3]Mises, *Human Action*, p. 207.

The problem of value measurement is indicated by the fact that not only do different people often value the same thing differently, but the same person might value a certain thing differently at different times. And under the operation of the law of diminishing marginal utility, a person will always value each additional unit of a given good less than the prior unit's value. If value were quantifiable and measurable, there would exist a standard unit of measure that would be unchanging. It is clear that there is no such immutable unit of measure of the value of a good when different people at the same time and the same person at different times often have divergent valuations of the same good.

Valuation necessarily is manifested in the act of choosing or preferring. One is able to say he values A more than either B or C, but he is unable to say quantifiably how much more he prefers A over B or C. He may qualitatively indicate that his preference of A over B is far more intense than his preference of A over C. In that case, he would be ranking his preferences from first to last in the order of A, C, and B. But this ranking is strictly an ordinal, and not a cardinal, use of numbers. The allocation of scarce resources cannot be based upon any alleged method of measuring their values; employment of particular increments of resources can be decided only through ranking one incremental choice over alternative incremental uses of the same or different resources. Resources, since they are means to consumer goods, derive their ranking from the relative importance of their ultimate products. A more detailed look at the subjective theory of value is presented in chapter 3.

Economic Calculation Through Money Prices

It is through the pricing process of the market that the *relative* importance of the various resources and consumer goods is translated into common terms in the form of money prices. Money emerges as the instrument of economic calculation. Money enables people to make economic calculations because it is the common medium of exchange. All goods and services that are bought and sold on the market are exchanged for sums of money. These money prices are not measurements of value. Money prices are exchange ratios that are expressive of the ranking of the valuations placed upon increments of goods at a given moment by the participants in market exchanges. Money prices are subject to continuous change because of the changeability of people's subjective valuations and because of changes in the supply of the particular goods and services. The propensity of humans to conceive of changes they deem improvements in their ways of doing things and in the means of attaining satisfaction prevents the emergence of permanently stable prices in the market economy.

Economic or monetary calculation is essentially a matter of providing a comparison between input and output, between sacrifice and result, for past or contemplated lines of resource utilization. It has been shown that calculations in kind, which must necessarily characterize technological computations, will not suffice for the task of economic allocations. Money prices related to particular quantities of goods and services permit the determination of money costs and money revenues, thereby shedding light on the desirability of specific resource employments.

Economic calculation includes both retrospective and prospective monetary calculations. Retrospective calculation is the determination of past monetary profit or loss, i.e., income, resulting from actions already taken and serves two purposes: (1) to the extent that the past is assumed to be indicative of the future, it has instructive value, and (2) the determination of monetary income reveals the extent to which the future capacity to produce can be maintained after current income is withdrawn. The latter function derives from the complementary concepts of capital and income, the ultimate mental tools of economic calculation, which are discussed in the next section. Prospective calculation, which might well be influenced by retrospective calculations of capital and income, is a matter of anticipating the money profit or loss expected to result from specific actions being contemplated. Note that all economic calculation deals with the future. As all action is meant to cause a beneficial change, all action is directed to the future, whether to the next hour, day, year, or longer. Every step along the path of resource utilization has a prospective orientation.

The Concepts of Capital and Income

The essence of modern economic activities is the devotion of resources to the process of production leading to the output of consumer goods and services. The entrepreneur-producer invests funds to acquire productive means by which he hopes to increase his monetary wealth. Through money prices the producer is able to ascertain numerically the economic significance of the factors employed for future production. The determinable amount of money equivalent devoted toward productive activities is called *capital*, and the aim to keep at least this amount intact is called capital maintenance. Mises defines capital in the following way:

> Capital is the sum of the money equivalent of all assets minus the sum of the money equivalent of all liabilities as dedicated at a definite date to the conduct of the operations of a definite business unit. It does not matter in what these assets may consist, whether they are pieces of land, buildings, equipment, tools of any kind and order, claims, receivables, cash or whatever.[4]

[4]Ibid., p. 262.

When productive efforts result in net assets whose money equivalent exceeds the capital devoted to such efforts, the business unit is said to have earned an income equal to that excess. The concept of income is the correlative of the concept of capital. Income is the amount that can be consumed without lowering the capital below the sum of the amount dedicated to the business at the start of a given period and any additional investments paid in during that period. If consumption is restricted to the amount of income, capital is maintained. If, on the other hand, consumption exceeds income, capital is not maintained; this difference is referred to as capital consumption. Capital accumulation takes place when consumption is less than the available income, that is, when a portion or all of income is saved. If the business fails to earn income and instead suffers a monetary loss, there is capital consumption, and capital is not maintained unless new funds are invested by the producer. Additional investments, in combination with income and consumption effects, make for either capital maintenance, capital accumulation, or a reduction in capital consumption. As Mises states, "Among the main tasks of economic calculation are those of establishing the magnitudes of income, saving, and capital consumption."[5]

Although capital may be embodied in produced factors of production (often called capital goods), the idea of capital refers to a concept existing only in the minds of individuals. Man is mentally aware of the monetary significance of the means to which he resorts for productive purposes. This concept is an element in economic calculation and provides a basis for appraising the results of future actions and for ordering subsequent steps of consumption and production through capital maintenance. The concrete capital goods are doomed to eventual dissipation; it is only the value of the capital fund that can be constantly preserved or maintained through a proper arrangement of consumption.

The establishment of the outcome of past actions involves the calculation of capital both prior to and after the actions. The comparison of these two calculations yields the determination of profit (income) or loss. This retrospective form of economic calculation provides a starting point in the planning of future actions to the extent that the actor deems the past an indicator of future developments. This point illustrates how the knowledge problem previously discussed is partly resolved.

In addition to serving instructive aims, the determination of profit or loss resulting from past actions provides the only means by which the actor or actors can ascertain whether or not the capacity of the business unit to produce in the future has been impaired. Like anyone else, producers are interested in attaining the satisfaction of their personal wants, and the

[5]Ibid., p. 261.

calculation of profit or loss reveals the extent to which they can enjoy consumption expenditures without encroaching on the capital base necessary to continue productive operations at a level comparable to that of the past. This calculation may show that additional investment is required in order to offset the dissipation of capital as a result of unprofitable operations or to achieve desired capital accumulation. And the most recent determination of capital affords a point of comparison for the calculation of profit or loss resulting from actions taken in the succeeding period. Thus retrospective economic calculation is significant only because it facilitates the planning of future actions; without this use it would be merely dead history.

Every productive undertaking is guided by the calculation of anticipated future costs and proceeds expected to result from the project or activity. The determination of past revenues and costs may be of substantial assistance in the projection of these results. For most entrepreneur-producers, only those actions will be pursued that promise a monetary output that sufficiently exceeds the expected monetary input, including capital dissipation, necessary to carry them out.[6] Resources then are directed into their most profitable uses by means of anticipatory calculations built on expected prices for various goods and services. Mises has made clear the overriding significance of monetary calculation:

> Monetary calculation is the guiding star of action under the social system of division of labor. It is the compass of the man embarking upon production. He calculates in order to distinguish the remunerative lines of production from the unprofitable ones, those of which the sovereign consumers are likely to approve from those of which they are likely to disapprove. Every single step of entrepreneurial activities is subject to scrutiny by monetary calculation. The premeditation of planned action becomes commercial precalculation of expected costs and expected proceeds. The retrospective establishment of the outcome of past action becomes accounting of profit and loss.[7]

It warrants reiteration at this point that economic or monetary calculation is not a process of measurement. Monetary numbers provide no standard unit of value. The infinite possible uses of productive resources dictate that choices or preferences, not value measurement, characterize the nature of the economic problem. Monetary calculations, through past

---

[6]This emphasis on profit-seeking behavior in no way precludes actions in the face of expected resultant money losses. Nonpecuniary benefits anticipated can serve to justify, from the viewpoint of the actor, money losses. Ultimate values are always personal and subjective. However, monetary calculation may still be of significance under such circumstances.
[7]Ibid., p. 229.

and anticipated market prices, indicate preferences or the relative importance of alternative undertakings.

Risk and Uncertainty

There is no precision in economic calculation because of the uncertain
future that pervades all activities in the market economy. Predicted
future costs and revenues are anticipations on the part of the
entrepreneur-producer, who possesses no superhuman ability to know the
future. This uncertainty no less affects the retrospective calculation of
profit and loss because the most recent calculation of capital is tenuously
based on a money equivalence that the future may not uphold. An individual decision maker is unable to know precisely the future preferences
of consumers, the future changes in technology, the future plans and actions of other producers, and the infinite number of other external events
that will occur in the future. The gathering of empirical data as is done in
establishing actuarial tables is not sufficient for the purposes of entrepreneurial activities in the market economy. Actuarial science is
predicated on determining classes of homogeneous events. Each class is
made up of a large number of past similar events that are subject to a
statistical analysis that reveals the percentage of instances a given event
has transpired. But the preponderance of the entrepreneur's dealings is
not with matters of a homogeneous nature. To the extent that he does concern himself with actuarially describable events, he resorts to insurance in
order to recognize the probable cost of detrimental happenings. But most
of his concerns are of such a comparatively rare nature that the grouping
or categorizing of them into classes for the purposes of computing class
probabilities is impossible.

Frank Knight developed this idea in distinguishing between risk and
uncertainty.[8] Risk is subject to numerical computation based on statistical
data pertaining to a large number of similar events that are expected to
recur. This is the nature of actuarial probabilities. Uncertainty relates to
situations that are unique; each situation is a case in itself as opposed to
being a member of a class or large number of homogeneous events or circumstances. Uncertainty is not numerically calculable because of the lack
of sufficient past experiences relating to the particular set of circumstances being considered.[9] Comprehensive empirical data are not
available in the varied classifications necessary to permit calculating the

[8]Frank A. Knight, *Risk, Uncertainty and Profit* (New York: Augustus M. Kelley, 1964).
[9]So-called subjective probability is a euphemism and always involves using numbers to represent a *judgment* of the likelihood of a given result occurring. Its name is an unfortunate mis-
use of words insofar as it connotes anything independently calculable or scientific.

probability of success for each of the innumerable ventures that are underway. Knight explains the problem this way:

> The liability of opinion or estimate to error must be radically distinguished from the probability or chance of either type (a priori and statistical), for there is no possibility of forming *in any way* groups of instances of sufficient homogeneity to make possible a quantitative determination of true probability. Business decisions, for example, deal with situations which are far too unique, generally speaking, for any sort of statistical tabulation to have any value for guidance. The conception of an objectively measurable probability or chance is simply inapplicable....[10]

Uncertainty is the overwhelming obstacle that each entrepreneur-producer faces in the market economy, and his attempt to foresee the future is a subjective matter that escapes mathematical equations and formulae. The businessman is not dealing with objects whose behavior is predictable as is a physicist or engineer. The object of the producer's attention are the wants of other people and the plans of other producers; it is not possible to know what changes they will undergo. The unexpected innovations and applied inventions on the part of competing producers have often spelled the downfall of less enterprising businesses. The changeability of customers' preferences and of resource availabilities are persistent problems confronting the producer. The uncertainty is primarily due to the unpredictability of the actions of other people. This is the central theme of the following remarks by Mises:

> In the real world acting man is faced with the fact that there are fellow men acting on their own behalf as he himself acts. The necessity to adjust his actions to other people's actions makes him a speculator for whom success and failure depend on his greater or lesser ability to understand the future. Every action is speculation. There is in the course of human events no stability and consequently no safety.[11]

This does not mean that the future is so uncertain that every business action is a gamble or that each situation is so unusual that there exists no basis for planned action. Experience provides an invaluable guide to action. Past prices are the starting point for predicting future prices. However, for the problems of the entrepreneur-producer, experience is too diverse and complex to enable him to quantify the probability of the success of alternative actions. In the market economy there are no fixed relations. The producer's reliance on past experience is necessarily judgmental and qualitative.

[10]Ibid., pp. 226, 231.
[11]Mises, *Human Action*, p. 113.

Since all anticipatory economic calculation deals with an uncertain future, all such calculations are tenuous and indefinite. Because no entrepreneur can know the future, errors in anticipations are inevitable, and success or profit comes to those whose foresight is the least erroneous or most nearly correct. Even the capital arising from the results of past events and transactions and used in determining past profits is but an interim level of wealth since its permanence is not assured in an uncertain future. Mises describes the tenuousness of the figures reported in business financial statements:

> The main thing in balance sheets and in profit-and-loss statements is the evaluation of assets and liabilities not embodied in cash. All such balances and statements are virtually interim balances and interim statements. They describe as well as possible the state of affairs at an arbitrarily chosen instant while life and action go on and do not stop....[12]

Monetary calculation may lack preciseness and certainty, but that does not mean it does not fulfill its task of guiding future actions according to a producer's view of what the future want-satisfactions of other people will be. It is not the fault of the system of economic calculation that uncertain calculations exist. They arise necessarily because human action always occurs in the face of an uncertain future. Under a social organization with an extensive division of labor, producers require a means of calculation on the basis of a common denominator. Monetary calculation affords this means, although it is not definite or certain. Resources are directed to those uses that the owner deems the most promising and remunerative as indicated by his money calculations. Monetary calculation is possible only in a market economy in which the factors of production can be related to money prices. There can be no monetary calculation in a barter economy or on Robinson Crusoe's island. Even socialist theorists have admitted that the allocation of productive resources in a socialized economy would require the establishment of money prices by the central authorities in order to correct discrepancies between supply and demand.

The Rationalizing Effect of Monetary Calculation

The recognition of the significance of economic calculation has not been restricted to Austrian economists. Max Weber attributed to the tool of monetary calculation or capital accounting the dominant rationalizing influence in the technological development of western capitalism:

> ...it is one of the fundamental characteristics of an individualistic

---

[12]Ibid., pp. 214.

capitalistic economy that it is rationalized on the basis of rigorous calculation, directed with foresight and caution toward the economic success which is sought in sharp contrast to the hand-to-mouth existence of the peasant, and to the privileged traditionalism of the guild craftsman and of the adventurers' capitalism, oriented to the exploitation of political opportunities and irrational speculation.[13]

The fact that what is called the technological development of modern times has been so largely oriented economically to profit making is one of the fundamental facts of the history of technology ... Had not rational calculation formed the basis of economic activity, had there not been certain very particular conditions in its economic background, rational technology could never have come in existence.[14]

It is only in the modern Western World that rational capitalistic enterprises with fixed capital, free labour, the rational specialization and combination of functions, and the allocation of productive functions on the basis of capitalistic enterprises, bound together in a market economy, are to be found.[15]

Mises has also recognized the pre-eminence of economic calculation:
No other distinction is of greater significance, both for human life and for the study of human action, than that between calculable action and noncalculable action. Modern civilization is above all characterized by the fact that it has elaborated a method which makes the use of arithmetic possible in a broad field of activities. This is what people have in mind when attributing to it the—not very expedient and often misleading—epithet of rationality. . . . Economic calculation is the fundamental issue in the comprehension of all problems commonly called economic.[16]

The instruments of money and monetary calculation are the means by which versatile and diversified resources can be rationally allocated to the satisfaction of urgent wants. The advances of technology are dependent on the guidance offered by such means. The great advantages of the division of labor could not have been realized without the calculations made possible in common terms by a common medium of exchange and its correlative, money prices.

And yet economic calculation is not without its limitations. Those things that cannot be bought and sold are outside the realm of monetary calculation. A man's devotion to good character or to another person may not be subject to compromise at any price. In a society that forbids

---

[13]Max Weber, *The Protestant Ethic and The Spirit of Capitalism* (New York: Charles Scribner's Sons, 1958), p. 76.

[14]Ibid., p. 163.

[15]Ibid., p. 297.

[16]Mises, *Human Action*, p. 199.

slavery, human life has no money price. A person may own something that he so cherishes for its beauty or for sentimental reasons that he would not exchange it for any amount of money. Such matters cannot be related to money prices. But the existence of these exceptions does not hinder the effectiveness of money prices in guiding the utilization of the vast amount of goods and services that do not fall outside the pale of market activities.

Coordinative Communication Through Market Prices

In addition to the need for a common denominator for calculation purposes, we have seen that another requirement of social cooperation based on specialization and division of labor and knowledge is for a means by which the multitude of individual plans and actions can be coordinated into a consistent pattern. The interrelationship of specialized activities demands a system of appraising decision makers of changes relevant to their activities. Each decentralized planner cannot make decisions strictly on the basis of his awareness of his immediate surroundings. His decisions need to be harmonized with those of other planners so that the larger economic system operates as smoothly and effectively as possible.

Money prices are the medium through which the communication of necessary information is made to coordinate effectively the actions of individual planners. As Hayek has pointed out, each particular decision maker does not need to know *all* the facts pertaining to the changes in resource usage. What is relevant to each is "how much more or less urgently wanted are the alternative things he produces or uses."[17] The economic question is always a question of the relative importance of specific things available for the satisfaction of human wants. Each planner does not usually need to know why the relative importance of the things that he uses or produces has changed. What he does need is some indication of the extent to which its relative importance has been altered. The crucial objective of such information is to see that each individual planner acts in the light of changes in the relative importance of the things with which he is concerned. Market prices at any moment reflect the relative importance most recently ascribed at the margin to goods and services exchanged on the market. Thus changes in the relative importance of goods and services are reflected in changes in their money prices.

The coordinating function performed by the price system can be illustrated by assuming a sudden shortage of some resource. Those people who will eventually solve the problem of the shortage do not need to understand its cause. The price of a unit of the resource will be driven up-

---

[17]Hayek, "The Use of Knowledge in Society," *Individualism and Economic Order* (Chicago: University of Chicago Press, 1948), p. 87.

ward as those who employ it in the most important usages, i.e., use it for the generation of products promising the highest return, outbid those producers who plan to use it in less remunerative products. The shortage has meant that the marginal uses of the resources that could be supplied before the advent of the shortage cannot be provided for as long as the shortage persists. The higher price successfully causes the curtailment of the employment of the resource in its marginal uses. Hayek has poignantly articulated the role of the price system:

> ...the marvel is that in a case like that of a scarcity of one raw material, without an order being issued, without more than perhaps a handful of people knowing the cause, tens of thousands of people whose identity could not be ascertained by months of investigation, are made to use the material or its products more sparingly; that is, they move in the right direction....I am convinced that if it were the result of deliberate human design, and if the people guided by the price changes understood that their decisions have significance far beyond their immediate aim, this mechanism would have been acclaimed as one of the greatest triumphs of the human mind. Its misfortune is the double one that it is not the product of human design and that the people guided by it usually do not know why they are made to do what they do.[18]

People far removed from the origin of the shortage are thereby led to plan and act in accordance with the fact that the supply of a particular factor of production has diminished. The higher price not only signals for adjustments in the quantities demanded; it also induces a search on the part of suppliers to increase the available supply of the resource. And to the extent this search is successful, the price of the good will fall accordingly, thereby indicating that the good is now available for employment in less remunerative lines. The price system operates in the same way to guide the actions of consumers in their acquisition of consumer goods and services. Hayek's further description of the effectiveness of the price system as a means of communicating information to dispersed decision makers is useful:

> ...The most significant fact about this system is the economy of knowledge with which it operates, or how little the individual participants need to know in order to be able to take the right action. In abbreviated form, by a kind of symbol, only the most essential information is passed on and passed on only to those concerned...a system of telecommunications which enables individual producers to watch merely the movement of a few pointers...in order to adjust their activities to changes of which they may never know more than is reflected in the price movement.[19]

[18]Ibid.
[19]Ibid.

Let us not fail to recognize that the effective operation of the price system can be thwarted by political interferences. Our current problems in oil and gasoline stem from the refusal on the part of those in power to allow the market system to function openly. The prices set by OPEC and by the Department of Energy are not prices freely set in the open market, and the distortions in supply and the gasoline lines are not the outcome of open-market decisions. Price controls hold prices down at points that cause frustration on the part of buyers, who are misled into thinking their demands at those prices can be met. These same price controls preclude the adequate search by oil producers to discover and market additional supplies of petroleum. Interferences with the price system perpetuate the problem of a "shortage" of fuel.

Money prices simultaneously fulfill the needs for a common denominator for calculation purposes and a process by which the individual decisions of dispersed people can be coordinated. Prices established on the market are coordinative precisely because they are a major factor taken into consideration in the economic calculations underlying the actions taken by various decision makers. Past prices are useful guides to the anticipation of prices expected to exist in the immediate future. Perceptions of opportunities for profitable alterations in economic activities engender actions that influence the eventual configuration of future prices. Through such changes in prices additional information is communicated to other market participants. The knowledge problem is further alleviated as such price signals now reflect the new decisions and induce others to plan their affairs in ways consistent with the new market data. The tendency for separate decisions to be consistent with one another was the natural outcome of establishing a medium of exchange that furnished to everyone a common denominator to be used for their economic calculations. Without a common denominator the need for coordinating the plans of various people would not be so great. The concomitant reliance on calculations in kind would significantly restrict the development of specialization and division of labor. Exchanges would be limited to pure barter relations. The rational allocation of scarce resources in a system of fruitful and extensive social cooperation is the great advantage emanating from a market economy and its counterpart, monetary calculation.

Suggested Readings

Knight, F. A. *Risk, Uncertainty and Profit*. New York: Augustus M. Kelley, 1964.
Mises, L. von. *Human Action: A Treatise on Economics*, 3rd rev. ed. Chicago: Regnery, 1963.

4. THE SUBJECTIVE THEORY OF VALUE

Satisfaction and Valuation

The explanation of all economic activity that takes place in the market economy ultimately rests on the subjective theory of value. The value of various consumer goods and services does not reside objectively and intrinsically in the things themselves, apart from the individual who is making an evaluation. His valuation is a subjective matter that even he cannot reduce to objective terms or measurement. Valuation consists in preferring a particular increment of a thing over increments of alternative things available; the outcome of valuation is the ranking of definite quantities of various goods and services with which the individual is concerned for purposes of decision and action. Theory resorts to the hypothetical concept of the scale of values in seeking to explain and understand the nature of human valuations. The ranking of alternative ends is determined by the person's expectations of satisfaction from each specific choice faced by him at any moment of decision. He will invariably select the alternative that he believes will yield him the greatest satisfaction.

The subjectiveness of valuation rests in the nature of satisfaction—satisfaction is subjective and not open to numerical measurement. The extent to which a thing gives satisfaction is always personal. People derive satisfaction from different goods and services; that is, all people are not alike in terms of the types of things that please them. Experience also demonstrates that a person's preferences vary from time to time. His ranking of alternative choices may undergo a reshuffling at any given moment. His scale of values may also be altered by deletions or additions.

To relate the matter of valuation to the individual person is not to suggest that each individual is concerned only with the satisfaction of his own appetites and needs. A person may find satisfaction or relief in helping another person. Satisfaction can be and often is derived from the attainment of altruistic as well as "selfish" motives. But the point remains that regardless of the form the satisfaction is to take, each choice arises from subjective valuation on the part of the particular person who is doing the choosing. The uneasiness that he seeks to remove is in his own mind, whether such uneasiness pertains to an immediate problem of his own or to a problem faced by someone else. His choice stems from the preference that he has for the removal of a particular uneasiness over another problem to which he could devote his attention.

The Principle of Marginal Utility

Valuation is always directed toward a definite quantity of a particular good or service. Choices and decisions are not concerned with the whole supply of a certain good or service. This marginal orientation was lacking in the classical economists' groping with the so-called paradox of value. They were unable to resolve the intriguing question of why diamonds had a higher price per unit than water when everyone knew that water was more useful and valuable than diamonds. Only through the principle of diminishing marginal utility could this conceptual dilemma be eliminated. Each additional unit of a particular good is devoted to a use that is less important and urgent than the use to which the preceding unit was applied.

To establish this principle one does not have to resort, as is sometimes done, to explanations of psychological or physiological satiety. The principle that a person will always apply a given unit of a good or service to the most pressing desire or need to which it relates is inherent in the concept of purposive action. Since each person prefers more satisfaction to less satisfaction, each succeeding unit obtained will be devoted to less and less important aims, given his scale of values at that time.

From the principle of diminishing marginal utility is derived an important law relating to the value of a unit of any good possessed in any particular quantity. The value of a unit of a given quantity of a particular good is determined by its usefulness in its least important use. To put the rule another way, the value of any unit of several units held of a given good is equal to the satisfaction that would be sacrificed if one unit were lost. Böhm-Bawerk illustrated the law by imagining a pioneer farmer who has reaped five sacks of grain from his harvest.[1] In planning carefully the use of this food supply, he first recognizes the essential need for a minimum amount of food to keep him alive until the following harvest. To this purpose he allots one sack of grain. A second sack will contribute to his enjoying full strength and complete health. A third sack will enable him to add some variety to his diet by using it for raising poultry. He decides to assign a fourth sack to the distillation of brandy; and finally, a fifth sack is to be devoted to the feeding of a group of parrots "whose antics give him pleasure."

The example depicts the operation of the principle of diminishing marginal utility. The farmer's plans for the sacks of grain proceed from the more important to the less important uses. The value of each sack of grain equals the satisfaction that the farmer expects to derive from being able to feed and enjoy his parrot friends. This is the satisfaction that he would surrender if he suffered the misfortune of losing one sack of grain. Since his sacks of grain are a homogeneous commodity, he does not have to go without any of the four more important uses because of his loss. He

[1]Eugen von Böhm-Bawerk, *Capital and Interest*, vol. 2, book 3 (South Holland: Libertarian Press, 1959), pp. 143–145.

28

will simply select the least important use in determining which part of his original plan cannot be effected. The value of a unit is determined by its marginal utility or satisfaction.

The principle of diminishing marginal utility and its complementary law of value resolve the paradox of value as exemplified by the discrepancy between the price of diamonds and the price of water. The element of scarcity in controlling the extent to which a particular commodity can be used holds the key. The relative abundance of water as compared with the availability of diamonds means that increments of water can be devoted to less and less important uses than those to which the limited amount of diamonds can be put. No one is ever in the predicament of having to choose between all water and all diamonds; thus there is no meaningful paradox. Prices arise in connection with definite amounts of goods and not in connection with whole categories of various goods.

If the amount of a good with which one is concerned is enlarged to encompass several of the smaller "units," the value theory is no less applicable. In this case, the larger amount becomes the marginal unit, and its valuation equals the sum of the various satisfactions that the larger amount would yield if broken down into incremental usages. For example, if our farmer is faced with giving up in one stroke three sacks of grain, his valuation of this package is not equal to three times the valuation or satisfaction attached to the maintenance of his parrots. He is not in the situation of valuing just one sack of grain. He will sacrifice the three least important uses of his sacks of grain, thereby devoting his remaining two sacks to meeting his essential food needs. The value of a "unit" of three sacks of grain equals the total satisfaction expected to be obtained from raising poultry, distilling brandy, and feeding parrots. This is the marginal satisfaction pertaining to the marginal unit of three sacks.

The size of the unit used is not important for the operation of value theory. It can be seen that if one were in the impossible position of having to rank all water and all diamonds, one would rate the former first and the latter second, disproving the existence of any paradox of value. It also follows that if the supply of a particular good is so large that some units go unused, the marginal utility of the good is zero; in such case, no value would be attached to any particular unit. The good would not belong to the realm of economics and could be expediently termed a "free" good. This is the case with the ordinary air that we breathe (although problems with air pollution have created certain situations that involve costly, not free, clean air).

Value and Exchange

In a modern economy the purpose of production is to yield goods and services to be used by people other than the producers themselves. This is the essence of specialization and division of labor. In a developed society, production for exchange overshadows production for immediate use. As a result, units of goods and services take on exchange value in addition to the use value that they may have for the producer. And with the overwhelming emphasis on production for exchange, the exchange value of produced goods looms as the value that is of real significance and relevance for most producers, while the use value of goods is the meaningful value for consumers.

It may appear that the concept of exchange value introduces a departure from the subjective theory of value, yet this is not the case. A unit of a given good derives its exchange value from the subjective value that is identified with the amount of some other good that can be obtained in exchange for it. This is true whether the good is to be exchanged directly for some other consumable good or for a certain amount of money. People wish to obtain other goods, including money, because they place a subjective valuation on such acquisitions. The value of a good as a means of exchange is based on the greatest satisfaction that the owner expects can be derived by giving up the good in exchange for some other good. The subjective value of the most desirable good or service that can be obtained in exchange is the basis of the value imputed to the possessed good.

Thus any particular good takes on both a use value and an exchange value. Each of these values reflects the satisfaction that can be expected to come by way of employing the good; the good can be employed either for direct use or as a means of obtaining some other good through outright exchange with another person. The controlling valuation for decision and action is always the greater of the two alternative satisfactions. If the good's use value exceeds its exchange value, the good will be put to direct use or held for eventual direct use, and its exchange value will be forgone. On the other hand, if its exchange value exceeds its use value, the good will be utilized for exchange purposes or held for possible exchange at some time in the future.

It should be understood that exchange value here refers to the *subjective* valuation placed by the owner on the good as a means of exchange. The expression "exchange value" is used frequently in the sense of the money price that can be obtained for a given good through its sale. In the context of the subjectivity of value, however, this objective money value would be evaluated subjectively in the same way that a noncash good obtainable through exchange would be evaluated.

Uses of Money

In most modern economies, money is primarily fiat money, and its use value in the sense of being employed for consumption purposes is virtually zero. However, where specie is used, money can have a considerable use value. For example, gold and silver can be melted down for jewelry, decoration, and dental applications. Incidents of converting money into other useful products are not common in modern economies; money is valued almost invariably for its exchangeability. Its great service is that it obviates the requirement for a coincidence of product wants among the parties to an exchange, as is required in cases of direct barter.[2]

There are three ways that a specific quantity of money can be put to immediate use. It can be used for the expenditure necessary to acquire another good or service to be used for consumption purposes. It can be spent for another good or service that is to be used in the productive process of effecting or fabricating a new good. In such case, an investment expenditure is made that is designed to yield future consumption or investment benefits through subsequent disposal or consumption of the produced good. Even wholesalers and retailers who bring about no change to the physical good itself affect a new good by placing it at a more accessible and convenient location. They are thereby engaged in the productive process, and the money spent to acquire the goods stocked is expended for production as opposed to consumption purposes.

The third use is to add the money to one's cash balance to help pay for future exchange transactions. The fact that a person holds a certain amount of money at a given moment indicates that he values the money more than those things that he could obtain in exchange for it. Yet holding an amount of money at a given moment does not alter the fact that money is valued for its exchangeability. It merely shows that being prepared for later exchanges is valued more highly than making exchanges now. The satisfaction arising from an increased cash supply is often manifested in a feeling of greater security. This valuation springs from the belief that in the future one will be better able to meet his needs by spending his accumulated cash balance. That a money asset yields a service or satisfaction and thus is not sterile and unproductive—as has been widely held in the study of economics since the days of Aristotle—has been elucidated by Professor W. H. Hutt.[3]

The principle of diminishing marginal utility is no less applicable to money than to other commodities. Units of money are utilized in such a way that the most urgent goals or needs are met first. Because of the particularly easy divisibility of money, such allocations are made in more incremental steps than is the case with any other commodity. The marginal

---

[2]In a later section the explanation of modern day inflation as the result of governmental debasement of money through credit expansion will be presented.

[3]See his essay, "The Yield from Money Held," in *On Freedom and Free Enterprise*, ed. Mary Sennholz (Princeton: D. Van Nostrand Co., Inc., 1956), pp. 196–216.

utility of money, then, equals the least highly valued use that the given unit serves. Just as in the case of the farmer's five sacks of grain, the satisfaction derived from a unit of money is the satisfaction that would be sacrificed if a unit were lost. The incidence of the loss will always be on the least important use that a unit was intended to serve. Yet this sacrifice is the most important use to which the marginal unit could be put. A person will thus allocate his money among consumption expenditures, production expenditures, and increases in his cash balance in terms of his scale of values or preferences.

Use and Exchange Value in the Market Economy

An important characteristic of the use of commodities, including money, in the productive process under a system of social cooperation is that the user is not concerned only with his own satisfactions or preferences. Since he is engaged in the generation of goods and services that are to be used by other people, the exchange value of the commodities depends on the relative preferences of the other people after the completion of the production process. The number of dollars that the producer anticipates will be the result of his productive efforts hinges ultimately on his perception of the values of other persons.

In a world of certainty, there would be no difficulty in arriving at a money appraisal for the group of employed goods and services. In the modern market economy, however, only in the few cases of guaranteed and contracted sales is the money outcome of certain productive efforts relatively certain. And even in those few cases the invested resources are usually of a scope exceeding what would be required to meet the contracted sales, indicating that the producer is banking on the occurrence of sales not yet contracted. The whole task of having to produce to suit the wants of other persons in the face of an uncertain future is the essence of entrepreneurship.

It can be seen that in the market economy, characterized by the production of goods and services for subsequent exchange by a common medium of exchange, both use and exchange values are a vital part of the economic process. For the ultimate users of goods and services, the consumers, the satisfaction arising from consumption is the source of value or utility. For producers, the goods and services devoted to production are meaningful only in terms of the money and its exchange value, which they expect to generate from the sale of their product. But the crucial point to remember in distinguishing between these two values is that the exchange value of any productive good tends to be connected with the use value that the consumers attach to its end product. The amount of money that consumers can be expected to allocate to various consumer goods and services is strongly influenced by their subjective preferences. It is this anticipated money inflow that provides the basis for arriving at an exchange value for goods and services devoted to production. An explanation of how the prices of productive resources tend to be derived from the prices of consumer goods will be offered in a later section.

The Pervasiveness of Subjective Valuation

Subjective valuation underlies all economic activity. Money is not a measure of value; quite the contrary, money is imputed a subjective value as a means of possessing other things. Any subjective valuation is immeasurable and is manifested only through specific choices and actions. Any particular choice is indicative of the decision maker's preference over all alternative courses of action considered during the time of decision. That this preference can be inferred from his actions does not mean that anything more than a preference is implied. As Rothbard has stated, "We deduce the existence of a specific value scale on the basis of the real act; we have no knowledge of that part of a value scale that is not revealed in real action."[4]

There is no way to measure quantitatively the satisfaction that the actor associates with his choice. Every choice requires rejection of the expected satisfaction from other possible choices; the highest ranked alternative forgone is the cost of any given decision. Benefits and costs are ultimately subjective. Every decision is predicated on the assumption that its benefits will exceed the advantages of the next best course of action; this is the background of every exchange. There is no such thing as an equal exchange. At the point of exchange, both buyer and seller consider themselves to be better off as a result of the exchange. In a system of extensive specialization and division of labor, most goods are produced for exchange. Specialized producers have little, if any, direct use for the goods they have produced; under the principle of diminishing marginal utility, the marginal utility of a unit of production is virtually zero as far as they are concerned. They place a higher valuation on the money that they can get for their goods. On the other hand, consumers or buyers value the goods obtained more highly than the money spent to acquire them. Exchanges can occur only when there are differences between the subjective valuations expressed by the parties of the exchanges.

The failure to consider this subjective orientation led to the unfortunate notion of the "economic man," which depicted every participant in the market economy as relentlessly seeking at every turn to maximize his monetary position. This idea is unrealistic because what people actually

[4]Murray N. Rothbard, *Man, Economy, and State* (Princeton: D. Van Nostrand Co., Inc.), I, 224.

seek in every action is a maximum psychic or subjective profit.

There are numerous examples of people forgoing additional monetary wealth because they deem the "cost" to be greater than its worth. There are investors who resist monetarily rewarding investments in industries whose products they find objectionable. Marketers have recognized that consumers sometimes consider factors besides the purchasable good and its related price. The availability of parking, the courtesy of clerks, and "store personality" now receive attention in discussions of merchandising. Wealthy entrepreneurs who continue to involve themselves in profit making even in their old age are undoubtedly motivated in many cases by something besides money. People often consider factors in addition to wages in deciding on a career or particular job.

The point of these examples is to demonstrate that people are not "economic men" in the classical sense and that money is not the ultimate basis of valuation. Even when dealing with money matters, people do not calculate monetarily in utmost detail every step and decision. They maximize subjectively but not momentarily, because monetary calculation must be sacrificed when its requirements on time and energy are recognized. Böhm-Bawerk dealt with this point:

> If anyone insisted on deliberating with maximum scrupulousness every one of the economic acts he undertakes every day, if he insisted on rendering a judgment of value throughout to the last detail concerning the most trifling good that he has to deal with by way of receipt or expenditure, by utilization or consumption, such a person would be too much occupied with reckoning and deliberating to call his life his own. The correct maxim and the one which would be observed in economic life is "Be no more accurate than it pays to be." In really important things, be really exact; in moderately important things be moderately exact; in the myriad trifles of everyday economic life, just make the roughest sort of valuation.[5]

It can be stated, however, that, other things being equal, people do strive to maximize their monetary position in choosing among alternative courses of action. A person will choose the alternative that promises to maximize his monetary position as long as he is indifferent to the non-monetary factors pertaining to the alternatives. In a money economy it is through the common medium of exchange that people are able to acquire most of those goods that yield them satisfaction. By maximizing their monetary position, they are able to command more goods and services from the market than they could with less money. This should not be misconstrued as meaning that all individuals ultimately seek maximum monetary wealth. The fervent pleas of participants in fund-raising endeavors whose stated objectives are to help the crippled surely are not

[5]Böhm-Bawerk, *Capital and Interest*, p. 202.

symptoms of greed. Money is the means by which many desired ends can be achieved.

A person will accept a less than maximum monetary position only when the satisfaction obtained from nonmonetary factors relating to another choice more than offsets the satisfaction associated with the money. The role of nonmonetary factors is likely to be greater with regard to the decisions of employment than with regard to those decisions relating to investment and consumption expenditures. Investors generally desire to maximize the financial return on their investment; consumers generally desire to acquire goods at the lowest possible prices.

Thus, despite the subjectivity of benefits and costs, the terms *money revenues* and *money costs* are meaningful references to the monetary inflows and outflows that arise in connection with productive activities. Regardless of the nonmonetary factors that are important to a given producer, his monetary position or outcome is also important to him insofar as he desires to continue to purchase certain goods and services. This means he must give more than cursory attention to money costs and money revenues.

However, it must be stressed once more than these money calculations are not in any way measurements of value in the subjective sense. Rothbard has stressed the need to use the term *value* with care: "It is important to keep distinct the subjective use of the term in the sense of valuation and preference, as against the 'objective' use in the sense of purchasing power or price on the market."[6] Yet this should not preclude the expedient use of the terms *money revenues, money costs,* and money values or *money valuations* as they refer only to monetary calculations. They relate to the realm of economic calculation that is vital to the direction of productive efforts toward the generation of the most desired goods and services.

Suggested Readings

Kirzner, I. M. *Market Theory and the Price System,* pp. 45–62.

Menger, C. *Principles of Economics* (1871). Trans. Dingwall and B. Hoselitz. Glencoe, Ill.: Free Press, 1950, pp. 114–174.

Mises, L. von. *Human Action: A Treatise on Economics,* pp. 92–98, 119–142.

---

[6]Rothbard, *Man, Economy, and State,* p. 271. Mises has chosen to make the distinction by using the term valuation with the subjective meaning and the term appraisement in the "objective," monetary sense. Cf. *Human Action,* pp. 331–33. The terms value and valuation have been employed in the subjective sense throughout this section.

5. THE MARKET AND MARKET PRICES

The Nature of the Market

The tendency to ascribe to the market economy the characteristic of being something other than the events caused by the choices and actions of individuals is incorrect. The market arises as a result of the willingness of individuals to interact. Every development in the market is the outcome of purposive actions on the part of individuals who are seeking to improve their own state of affairs.

This process of economic interaction and cooperation is the essence of the market; the market is not something physical but a process. Through the consummation of market transactions, individuals seek to improve their situations, i.e., enhance their own subjective satisfactions. The prices that emerge in the market are not unexplainable; they always are the result of subjective valuations expressed by individuals who chose to buy or sell or to abstain from either action. Mises emphasizes the human quality of all market activities:

> It is customary to speak metaphorically of the automatic and anonymous forces actuating the "mechanism" of the market. In employing such metaphors people are ready to disregard the fact that the only factors directing the market and the determination of prices are purposive acts of men. There is no automatism; there are only men consciously and deliberately aiming at ends chosen. There are no mysterious mechanical forces; there is only the human will to remove uneasiness. There is no anonymity; there is I and you and Bill and Joe and all the rest. And each of us is both a producer and a consumer.... There is nothing inhuman or mystical with regard to the market. The market process is entirely a resultant of human actions. Every market phenomenon can be traced back to definite choices of the members of the market society.[1]

Price Determination—Consumer Goods

The Demand Side

The underlying purpose of all productive effort in the market economy is the generation of goods and services to be consumed. Money prices for consumer goods and services occur continuously as possession of these goods and services moves from the producer to the consumer. A market price is the exchange ratio or relationship between a particular good and the medium of exchange. Although the conventional supply and demand explanation of how equilibrium prices tend to be set in order to clear the

---

[1]Mises, *Human Action*, pp. 258, 315.

market of particular goods is legitimate, it is necessary to examine the real meaning behind the diagram of intersecting curves.

Each potential consumer allocates his money so that his most urgent wants are satisfied first. This means that for any particular good whose purchase he contemplates, there is a ranking within his scale of values. It must be remembered that his scale of values reflects the relative subjective importance that he attaches to each alternative use of his money. Each potential purchase has to compete with alternative potential purchases and with the possibility of his retaining his money. Thus an additional unit of a given consumable good will rank higher or lower than a given amount of money. If it is preferred over, say, six units of money, he is willing to purchase one unit of the good in exchange for six units of money. Conversely, if he prefers to retain six units of his money for some other use rather than acquire a unit of the good, he will not be willing to purchase it at a price of six money units.

Assume that he will pay six units of money for one unit of a given good. Assume also that his rankings entail his preference for a second unit of the good at any price between, say, four and one money units, and that at a price of one unit of money, he is willing to buy a third unit. This means that at a price of four, five, or six money units he will buy one unit; at a price of two or three units of money he is willing to buy two units of the good; and if the price reaches one, he wishes to acquire three units.

It is in this way that a hypothetical individual's so-called demand curve can be drawn illustratively for each particular good that he might consider buying at a given moment. At each possible price, he either purchases a certain quantity of the good or purchases none of it. Because of the diminishing marginal utility of the good, he will be willing to increase the quantity purchased only at lower and lower prices. This is the reason for drawing his demand curve downward-sloping to the right. The total demand for a particular good then becomes the summation of each prospective consumer's individual demand. And though each individual demand may be unique, each curve depicting an individual's demand will be downward-sloping to the right. Thus the curve depicting total demand for a particular good will have the same kind of slope, i.e., downward-sloping to the right.

What is crucial to the understanding of demand is that the principle of diminishing marginal utility is constantly operating in the consumer's purchasing decisions. Each additional unit of a given good is applied to a less important use than the former unit acquired. And while the marginal utility of the good continuously falls with each added unit, the marginal utility relating to the remaining money rises. Increases in quantity demanded must be accompanied by decreases in price.

Though the usual discussion of demand recognizes the subjective nature of a consumer's buying decisions, the supply side of price analysis invariably fails to be related to subjective value, despite the great importance of subjective valuations in the selling decisions of producers.

Each individual producer who has a certain stock of some consumer good ranks the units of the good in the same manner that a prospective consumer ranks his stock of money. There are three possible uses to which he can allocate his stock: He can use the good directly; he can sell it now for money; or he can retain the good for future sale. He will place subjective valuations on these different possibilities, devoting the various units to the most important usages. Based on this allocation, he ranks on his value scale each unit (remember the term "unit" can embrace any number of smaller increments) to be sold and the amount of money to be received in return. For each possible unit price he will be willing to sell either a certain quantity of the good or none of it. He will have to decide whether what he gives up is less or more valuable to him than the price he receives.

It is likely that to specialized producers the value of the good in direct use is virtually nil. If his valuation of the good for purposes of future sale is also slight, he will be willing to sell nearly all of his stock at a meager price per unit, provided that the marginal utility of money falls slowly as he obtains more of it. To the extent that he values using some units for purposes other than immediate sale, there will be some prices that are too low for him. In the absence of any compensating nonmonetary factors, in no case would he be willing to sell more units for lower prices per unit than for higher prices per unit.

If there is little value in not selling his entire stock of goods, his supply curve will be more or less vertical, meaning that at any possible price throughout the relevant range of his supply curve he is willing to sell all units of the good. Otherwise the curve will be upward-sloping to the right, indicating that as some units are sold, the marginal utility of the good increases in terms of the value of alternative uses, thereby requiring more money in exchange for additional units. The seller's supply curve will never be upward-sloping to the left.

Assume a seller has a stock of eight units of a particular good. If six units of money is more valuable to him than each of the units of the good, considering their alternative uses, then he will want to sell his entire stock at the unit price of six units of money. But suppose that at a price of five units of money he is willing to sell only six units of the good. Each of the two remaining units has a greater value to him than five units of money. At a price of four money units, he will sell only four units; at a price of three units of money, he is willing to sell but one unit of his good. And, at a price of one or two money units, he will not sell any of his stock of goods.

The law of marginal utility explains the behavior of this producer. The utility of a unit of his good in uses other than current sale rises as he decreases his stock. He insists on a greater amount of money in exchange for additional units. His selling decisions rest on his subjective valuations in the same way that the buying decisions of a given consumer depend on *his* scale of values.

A total supply curve for the good would entail the summation of all of the individual supply curves and, thus, its various segments would be either vertical or upward-sloping to the right.

The Tendency Toward Equilibrium Prices

The day-to-day tendency in the market is toward the establishment of an equilibrium price for each particular consumer good. Prevailing prices tend toward that price at which quantity supplied and quantity demanded are equal, a movement that attests to the price system's capacity to coordinate the actions of persons engaged in different activities. The typical depiction of this tendency on a graph shows the equilibrium price at the point at which the market supply-and-demand curves intersect. Any price above or below the equilibrium price cannot persist because such a price will result, respectively, in either frustrated sellers or frustrated buyers. Prices are reduced by sellers if the market price is too high to clear the quantity offered; prices are bid upward by buyers if the price is too low to induce sellers to offer a quantity ample enough to satisfy the buyers' demand.

Market rents for leased durable consumer goods are established by the same pricing process. Rents are prices paid for the service units obtained through the right to use someone else's property over a period of time. Thus there is a demand for and supply of services obtainable through leased goods. Rothbard has explained this market development in the following way:

> Since any good is bought only for the services that it can bestow, there is no reason why a certain period of service of a good may not be purchased. This can be done, of course, only where it is technically possible. Thus, the owner of a plot of land or of a sewing machine or of a house may "rent it out" for a certain period of time in exchange for money. While such hire may leave legal ownership of the good in the hands of the "landlord," the actual owner of the good's service for that period is the renter, or tenant.[2]

It should be mentioned at this point that there is a connection between the expected rental prices in the future and the purchase price of the good

[2]Rothbard, *Man, Economy, and State*, I, p. 170.

as a whole. The market price of the good tends to equal the present value of the expected future rentals. If the present value of expected future rentals is greater than the price of the good as a whole, more people will want to own the good as opposed to renting it. Meanwhile, present owners will be more reluctant to sell. This excess demand for the good will cause the price of the good to be bid upward toward the present value of future rentals. On the other hand, if the present value of expected rentals is less than the price of the good, fewer will want to buy the good and owners will want to sell rather than rent the good. This oversupply of the good causes its price to be lowered to come more in line with the present value of expected rentals, and thus price relations are established in the market through the same forces of supply and demand. Since prices are subject to change, the predicted future rentals are not simply a multiple of present rental prices. The relationship between the market price of the good and future rents is only a long-run tendency.

The explanation of what is going on in the pricing process is not served merely by diagrams, however. One has to think of the process in terms of acting individuals following their own particular subjective valuations. If the price is too high or too low relative to the equilibrating price, individuals behave purposefully to correct the situation. Every exchange requires two mutually benefited parties. As Mises has said, the process is not mechanical or inhuman.

When it is said that the market process tends to yield an equilibrium price for each good, no reference is being made to the pricing of all physically identical goods. If consumers view the offerings of a certain supplier as being different in some way from those of other sellers, the good is a different good for the purposes of economic analysis, even if its observable physical attributes are the same as those of other sellers' goods. What really counts is how consumers perceive the various supplies of goods brought before them. Similarly, goods situated a long distance away are not the same as goods a short distance from use. The "same good" means the units of the good are equally serviceable to the buyer. Goods that have to be transported from far away are less complete and, hence, less serviceable because transportation to point of acquisition is part of the production process.

Thus different market prices can prevail for goods that a hypothetical, neutral observer, focusing solely on physical qualities, would deem identical. This is what Mises means when he says that

> the market does not generate prices of land or motorcars in general nor wage rates in general, but prices for a certain piece of land and for a certain car and wage rates for a performance of a certain kind. It does not make any difference for the pricing process to what class the things exchanged are to be assigned from any point of view.

However they may differ in other regards, in the very act of exchange they are nothing but commodities, i.e., things valued on account of their power to remove felt uneasiness.[3]

It is important to emphasize in price analysis that the movement toward market equilibrium prices is a tendency that seldom reaches fruition because of the continuous changes that occur in people's subjective valuations and in the supply of each good. To assume that established prices will perpetuate themselves is to conceive value as objective and unchanging. But individuals, both buyers and sellers, experience constant change in their valuations, purposes, and acts. The very essence of action is change. The ceaseless changing of human choices and actions upsets the tendency in the market for the establishment of equilibrating prices. Yet, with the advent of every change in market data, the process sets out in a new direction toward a different equilibrium price. Price analysis resorts to the mental tool of equilibrium prices in order to explain the continuous tendency of the market process. Market prices are the result of the particular circumstances that existed at the time of their occurrence.

The changeability of prices makes inappropriate any reference in the strict sense to prices as present or current prices. As Mises says, "prices are either prices of the past or expected prices of the future."[4] To refer to prices as "current" prices is to say that immediate future prices will be the same as the historical prices of the most recent past, say half an hour ago. Since prices generally are not violently restructured from moment to moment in the market, recent past prices are useful starting points in the projection of future prices. But it is future prices that are of primary significance to each actor. Past prices convey directly no certain *knowledge* about future prices.

The Irrelevance of Past Costs

It should be stressed that this analysis applies to goods already produced; these are the goods that enter into the day-to-day pricing of consumer goods. This is the reason the analysis needs to make no reference to the seller's money costs of production. The individual seller's costs were shown to relate to his subjective scale of values—that is, to his own valuation of the good in its next best alternative use of either direct use or future sale. Once the goods have been produced, his past money costs are irrelevant to deciding how to use these goods. As Thirlby has said, "Cost is ephemeral. The cost involved in a particular decision loses its significance with the making of a decision because the decision displaces the alter-

---

[3]Mises, *Human Action*, p. 393.
[4]Ibid., p. 217.
[5]G. F. Thirlby, "The Subjective Theory of Value and Accounting 'Cost,'" *Economica* (February 1946): 34.

native course of action."[5] Jevons stressed the same truth when he stated, "In commerce bygones are forever bygones and we are always starting clear at each moment, judging the value of things with a view to future utility. Industry is essentially prospective not retrospective."[6] The seller's task is to make the best of his situation in light of his possessing a certain stock of goods.

Thus it is not correct to say that prices are determined by demand and by money costs. Money costs enter into the seller's decisions about the undertaking of production.[7] This matter of planning production is treated in chapter 5. Once the goods are produced, only subjective valuations expressed by individual buyers and sellers relating to these goods and to their exchange ratios in money terms are effective in the establishment of market prices.

The Preeminence of Consumer Valuations

In the final analysis the subjective valuations of the consumers are the principal factor in the determination of market prices of consumer goods in the advanced market economy. It can be seen that the subjective valuations of any given seller in possession of a stock of goods ultimately are concerned with generating the greatest amount of money revenues through the sale of the goods. This is not to say that money measures his satisfaction in any way; it simply recognizes the fact that more money means more to him than does less money in a situation in which non-monetary factors have already been considered. His preference concerning nonmonetary factors would have been weighed in his decision to undertake the production of the given goods. With more money he is able to acquire more of those things that yield him satisfaction.

Now to reduce the object of his valuations to the money obtainable from consumers is to render insignificant in his scale of values one possible use of the goods: direct use of the goods by the seller himself as opposed to their sale. To justify the subservience of use value to exchange value, one needs only to regard the predicament of a specialized producer in the advanced market economy: He simply will have little direct use for the stock of a particular good. The seller of shoes is not likely to desire to retain a large quantity of shoes for consumption purposes. His only recourse is eventually to exchange them for the best possible price. He will consider the price for which he can currently exchange the shoes as well as the price he expects to be realizable in the future.

---

[6]William Stanley Jevons, *The Theory of Political Economy*, 3rd ed. (London: MacMillan & Co., 1888), p. 164.
[7]Buchanan makes the useful distinction between "choice-influencing" and "choice-influenced" cost. In this sense, actual money costs emerge as choice-influenced costs. See James M. Buchanan, *Cost and Choice* (Chicago: Markham Publishing Co., 1969), pp. 44, 45.

42   These are the concerns of his subjective valuations, and his own time preference will enter into the valuation of future prices. If he places virtually no value on use value or future exchange value, as reflected by a vertical supply curve, the market price will equal that price necessary to clear the market. On the other hand, if expected prices of the future are high enough to deter current sale of all the goods at any price, as evidenced by a supply curve with upward-sloping segments, his valuation of his goods for future sales purposes is no less dependent on consumer evaluations as he anticipates them to be reflected in future money prices. And eventually, when these goods currently being held back at lower prices are offered for sale, the price willingly paid by consumers will be the determining factor. Exchange value is by definition derived from the valuations of those who are to receive the good in exchange and who willingly pay money for it.

Suggested Readings

Mises, L. von. *Human Action: A Treatise on Economics*, pp. 257–289 and pp. 327–397.

Rothbard, M. N. *Man, Economy, and State: A Treatise on Economic Principles.* New York: Van Nostrand, 1962, pp. 160–272.

6. PRODUCTION IN AN EVENLY ROTATING ECONOMY

We must now explain how scarce resources are allocated in the production of various consumer goods in the market economy. The generation of consumer goods, as will be shown, is a complex process in which the production of numerous goods used to make other goods, often called capital goods, plays an essential role. Production requires the creation of capital goods to be used in further production as well as the final goods designed to please the consumer. One can readily observe that in our economy the decisively preponderant form of economic activity is the production of intermediate or capital goods as opposed to final consumption goods. Nature does not bestow an abundance of goods on man in immediately consumable forms. With the exception of the air (and this exception is not everywhere applicable), there is hardly any good that nature supplies that cannot be made far more useful through the application of some productive effort. The question is not whether there should be production, but to what ends should production be directed so that the most desirable goods and services are produced.

Resource Pricing in an Evenly Rotating Economy (ERE)

In order for the owners of productive factors to be willing to contribute resources to the productive process of the market, there must be some means by which they can share in the output arising from production. Their participation is achieved through the price system. Particular units of productive factors are exchanged for specific quantities of money through supply-and-demand forces in the same way that consumer goods are bought and sold. However, there is one crucial difference between the pricing of consumer goods and productive factors: Consumer goods are evaluated directly by consumers as ends or ultimate sources of satisfaction, but consumers do not evaluate the resources used to generate the final goods. It should be clear that effective allocation of scarce resources requires a system in which specific employments are considered in terms of the relative importance of alternative results. If certain ends or consumer goods are more important than others, then resources versatile enough to serve a variety of ends should be directed to the creation of the most important ones. An explanation of the pricing of units of resources will show how this goal is accomplished.

The concept of an imaginary economy devoid of change in technology, resources, and tastes, an economy in which the same steps of production and consumption are repeated over and over, is useful in understanding the nature of the pricing of resource units in the real world of continuous change. Rothbard has called such an economy an evenly rotating economy, or ERE. In the ERE, each producer, given his predicament of owning some resources and bidding for units of particular resources, would be able to impute to a given resource unit the money value of its contribution to the final product because he would know in advance the monetary result of particular production decisions. He would not encounter the uncertainty arising from changing economic conditions. Past results would exactly predict future results.

The unit price of each type of resource would equal the discounted value of its marginal contribution to product value. (The discount relates to a margin reflecting time preference or interest, a matter to be discussed at a later point). This price would apply to the resource in all of its various lines of employment to the extent that the resource owners were indifferent to the nonmonetary factors relating to the different lines. The resource could not earn more in one line than in another because resource owners would have shifted their factor to the more remunerative lines. This shift would have driven the factor price down in the attractive employments and caused the price to rise in those abandoned lines. Prices of homogeneous factors would become equal in all employments.

This uniform price would be equated to the resource's marginal value product, which would thus be the same in all lines of employment. Producers would not tolerate any discrepancy between a factor's price and its contribution to product value. If a resource had been receiving a price lower than its marginal value product, producers would have increased the use of the resource in these outputs so that its unit price would be bid upward but not in excess of its contribution to productive value. Conversely, if a resource unit had been paid a price higher than its marginal value product, employment of the resource would have fallen off in those lines at least until the price ceased to exceed the factor's contribution to product revenues. The price of a durable factor would be derived from and equal to the summation of the marginal value products of its specific service units to be used over time. Durable resources, then, could be purchased or rented in the ERE according to the value imputed to the service units to be derived.

Thus in the evenly rotating economy the price of each product would (except for the interest factor) equal the summation of the marginal value products of its complementary factors of production. For each producer, total money revenues (excluding interest) would equal total money costs. Adjustments leading up to the ERE would have eliminated all instances of profit and loss. The continuous stability and certainty of an evenly rotating economy would preclude the need for further adjustments or changes in resource allocation. Each factor would be allocated to various uses so that its marginal product contribution would be the same in each use. With perfect knowledge about the future, producers would make no mistakes about imputing product values to resource values. What is of extreme importance here is that the influence is from product price back to factor price, and not the other way around. Means derive their importance from the ends or results they effect. Here lies the key to effective resource utilization. Yet, the erroneous notion that factor costs determine product prices has widespread acceptance.

Only those factor units whose marginal effect on product value could be isolable and hence determinable would be subject to the competitive forces that would set resource prices equal to discounted marginal value product. This means that determinate pricing would require the existence of versatile, relatively nonspecific factors whose multiple uses set the competitive process in motion as producers bid for the factors' employment in various lines of production. A price emerges on the market for a particular resource because producers compete for its employment in alternative uses. If products were produced by strictly specific resources, then the market could establish only cumulative prices for each combinational group of resource factors, and each price would represent the monetary value of the common product. Prices are determinate for absolutely specific resources in those situations in which the production process uses no more than one specific resource. As a result of the bidding of competitive producers, such prices of specific resources equal the residual difference between the final product price and the sum of the prices of the nonspecific factors.

Cumulative residual prices will prevail on the market in connection with those processes in which more than one specific resource is required. In such cases, the amount singly paid to each specific factor is established only through the process of bargaining among the separate owners of the specific factors. Prices of particular factors emerge only when producers compete for their use in alternative lines of production or when there is only one specific resource in each productive process, thereby imputing marginal value to the particular factor's units.

It is important to realize that the imputation of value to factors of production on the part of producers is done only on an incremental or marginal basis. In hiring or purchasing productive services, the producer always makes his decision in terms of the added advantage of the additional factor. This does not mean that he deals with infinitesimal increments. For example, his marginal unit may be fifty additional employees or four new machines, but he thinks in terms of his particular situation and bids for services in light of their expected marginal contribution. Rothbard has effectively dealt with this point:

> It is, then, clearly impossible to impute absolute "productivity" to any productive factor or class of factors. In the absolute sense, it is meaningless to try to impute productivity to any factor, since all the factors are necessary to the product. We can discuss productivity only in marginal terms, in terms of the productive contribution of a single unit of a factor, *given the existence of other factors.* This is precisely what entrepreneurs do on the market, adding and subtracting units of factors in an attempt to achieve the most profitable course of action.[1]

Just as the farmer's five sacks of grain were allocated to the most urgent uses first, so are the units of a productive factor. As additional units of any factor are employed in a given process or throughout the economy, the marginal value product declines. The decline in the marginal value product is enhanced as a result of the law of diminishing returns, which holds that in the employment of any variable factor to a fixed factor, marginal physical productivity begins to fall at a certain point. This means that, given the supply of a particular factor, the price per unit of that factor will be set equal to the marginal value product related to the last unit of supply. As each of the farmer's sacks of grain carried the same value equal to the value of the marginal use—feeding pet parrots—each unit of a particular factor is priced in the ERE equal to the marginal value product, which is the money value that would be sacrificed if one unit of the factor were lost.

This process of resource pricing would apply to factor service units, whether purchased on a limited scale through renting or on a greater scale through the purchase of whole factors. In the ERE, all factor service units would receive their marginal value product, and there would exist no reason for their being shifted to other lines of employment once this condition was reached. Each particular factor would have one unit price throughout the market. In each specific use the resource would be employed to the extent that its marginal value product was equal to its price, competitively established throughout its market. The demand curve for each factor in each particular use depicts its declining marginal value product; like the demand curve for consumers' goods, it would be downward-sloping to the right.

The supply curve for each productive resource in each line of use would be upward-sloping to the right, reflecting the fact that resource units, possessing a versatility of productiveness in alternative uses, would be shifted away from the given use to other uses at lower prices and would be attracted to the given use from alternative lines of employment at higher

[1]Rothbard, *Man, Economy, and State,* II, p. 520.

prices. The curve would probably be flatter for factors of labor than for land and capital goods factors because of the relatively greater degree of nonspecificity and flexibility in the nature of the labor resources.

Resource Supply, Entrepreneurial Activity, and Subjective Valuation

The theory of subjective value must not be overlooked in the discussion of factor supply curves. The owners of the units of factor service will subjectively determine the various quantities of service units that they are willing to offer to producers for each possible price per service unit in each particular use of the factor. They will weigh subjectively the monetary and nonmonetary results of committing the various possible quantities of service units to production. For example, the laborer will consider the value of leisure as well as other nonmonetary factors like working conditions in reaching his decision about employment. Those lines of work associated with significantly favorable nonmonetary characteristics would attract a greater number of workers than those characterized by noticeably unfavorable working conditions. Higher wage rates or prices than otherwise necessary would be paid those working in the generally disliked jobs; conversely, lower wages than otherwise required would be paid to those employed in the generally favored jobs.

These results are consistent with the principle of declining marginal value product for each particular use. Greater quantities of factors employed would tap decreasing marginal value products; lesser quantities would relate to higher marginal value products. Market supply curves for each factor in each particular use would show the summation of individual supply curves. The intersection of the market demand-and-supply curves would show the establishment of the equilibrium price for each factor in each particular line of employment, and this price would represent the marginal value product of a factor unit in that particular use. Such would be the endlessly prevailing price structure for units of productive resources in the evenly rotating economy.

In hiring or purchasing factors of production, the producer, like all other market participants, is acting on his own subjective value judgments.[2] His willingness to invest specific amounts of money or commit himself to the investment of amounts of money obtained from others, who likewise act on personal valuations, reflects his decision that taking

[2]Under the assumption of perfect knowledge posited with the ERE, there would be no place for the entrepreneur. This explains the absence here of the term used repeatedly in earlier sections, the "entrepreneur-producer." Nevertheless, the same point being made above concerning the relevance of subjective value is no less applicable to the entrepreneur-producer in the real world of uncertainty.

48

other actions instead would contribute less satisfaction to him than pursuing his business plan. His subjective evaluation of expected "money costs" and other forms of sacrifice, i.e., forgone alternative satisfaction or, in Buchanan's terms, his "choice-influencing" costs, is lower than the subjective value expected to be realized from the action chosen.

The Efficiency of Resource Allocation in an ERE

Note again that the monetary valuation of scarce economic resources would be equal to the value of their respective products so that an efficient allocation of resources would result. Resource prices, or money costs, would be derived from product prices. Economic calculation, afforded the producers through the structure of market prices, would provide the means through which resources could be employed consistent with the wishes and preferences of the consumers. *Ex post* and *ex ante* calculations would agree. In a world in which tastes, resources, and technology are constant, there would be no problem or difficulty in coordinating the different plans and actions of the various members of society. Everyone would know in advance the needs of tomorrow. For the purposes of economics, there would be perfect knowledge.

Production and Time

In an advanced economy the time between the inception of virtually every consumer good and its fruition is exceedingly long. In order to obtain goods that they desire and can consume, people are able to resort ultimately to only two types of productive resources, themselves and nature. Because either the goods that come from nature are not completely accessible to humans, or the resources of nature are not always usable in their natural state, humans inject their own efforts into the natural process. This productive effort transforms and combines the gifts of nature into more satisfactory goods. All such production must take place through time; thus, the fundamental and ultimate requirements for production are nature, man, and time.

Humans can combine their own efforts with the gifts of nature to produce consumable goods either directly or indirectly. Using the direct approach, a person applies his energies to a natural resource for immediate satisfaction, as in obtaining a drink of water from a stream. It was owing to the great contribution of Böhm-Bawerk that economic analysis recognized that production cannot occur without the passing of time, a recognition that was especially pertinent in connection with the indirect approach to production.[3] Under this second method, production first yields intermediate goods that are not consumable but rather are used to

[3]Böhm-Bawerk, *Capital and Interest*.

assist in further production efforts. These intermediate goods, known as producers' goods or capital goods, include tools, equipment, buildings, and all other produced means of production. An example of this indirect method, which Böhm-Bawerk called "roundabout production," is obtaining water to drink from the stream with a log hollowed out to make a bucket. The bucket could be used to make the acquisition of water easier by reducing the number of trips to the stream.

The advantage of roundabout or indirect production is not confined to making it easier to acquire goods that already exist in consumable form, such as water. A far greater advantage is its capacity to produce consumer goods that otherwise could never be made available. All modern conveniences such as cars, communications devices, refrigerators, eyeglasses, and countless others would be nonexistent were their production not preceded by the creation of tools and equipment. In an advanced economy, units of these capital goods are a significant part of the factors being purchased for production purposes. In the ERE, each particular type would be priced per service unit at an amount equal to its discounted marginal value product. The price of the whole capital good would equal the capitalization of its future marginal value products.

Time Preference and Interest

Because of the time-consuming element of production, the price paid each factor unit in the ERE is its discounted marginal value product and not its full marginal value product. The principle of time-preference, which holds that people prefer present goods to future goods, underlies the requirement that future marginal value products be discounted to their present values. People who save some of their purchasing power and invest in productive undertakings thereby forgo the enjoyment of consumption goods that that purchasing power could have obtained. They exchange present goods for future goods. When they purchase units of productive factors in the expectation of generating future purchasing power, i.e., future goods, they provide the former owners of these resources with a means to acquire present goods. However, since they prefer present goods over future goods, future goods are valued less in the present than are present goods, and it is this lesser value that is presently imputed to the marginal value product of each productive factor. This is why in an ERE producers would earn an interest income, the difference between the money value of consumer goods and the money value of productive resources purchased at earlier points in time.

In an advanced economy in which extensive usage of roundabout production processes is prominent, the interest factor is of utmost importance. Here rests the kernel of Böhm-Bawerk's devastating reply to Marx's exploitation theory, which maintained that capitalist-producers exploited the working class by paying them less than the value of their products. Marx was right in citing the emergence of a surplus value, but he was wrong in overlooking that rather than being a matter of exploitation, this discrepancy was partly the result of a natural and unavoidable phenomenon: interest.

In an ERE, the interest rate would be the same throughout the economy and in every productive stage because if interest rates were higher in certain industries or stages than in others, producers would shift to the more remunerative lines so that the differences would disappear as the result of competitive forces. In those industries or stages that producers abandon, the demand for productive resources falls, thereby reducing the prices of units of factors. This raises the discrepancy between marginal value product and money costs; hence the interest rate in those lines is increased. On the other hand, in those industries that attract additional investment, interest rates fall as a result of higher resource prices and the lower selling prices of finished goods.

This process of shifting investment would go on until the interest rate in every line of production became the same, at which point an evenly rotating economy would be reached. The higher the rate of interest, the more production efforts will be directed toward the production of consumer goods and the less saving available for more time-consuming production of future goods. A lower rate of interest indicates a lower discounting of future goods to present goods and is concomitant with greater savings and the opportunity to adopt more time-consuming processes of production.

Even Böhm-Bawerk, who played such a vital role in developing interest theory, committed the common error of attributing the interest factor to the productivity of capital goods. But interest can be explained completely by the principle of time-preference and does not arise only in connection with the employment of capital goods. The productivity of capital goods is already taken into consideration in determining which marginal value products should be discounted for the time period expected to elapse before the future goods become present goods. And this applies to all factors of production, not just capital goods. Mises says:

> The contribution of the complementary factors of production to the result of the process is the reason for their being considered as valuable; it explains the prices paid for them and is fully taken into account in the determination of these prices. No residuum is left that is not accounted for and could explain interest.[4]

Interest is not a return peculiarly characteristic of the use of capital

[4]Mises, *Human Action*, p. 530.

goods, as has often been contended. The classical association of interest only with capital goods is not tenable because interest permeates all economic activity in which present goods are furnished in exchange for future goods. Thus interest arises in consumer loans as well as producer loans. The phenomenon of interest operates as well in the price paid for land and labor whose benefits or proceeds are to be received in the future. In fact, if it were not for the element of time-preference, the prices of parcels of land would be infinite.

Suggested Readings

Mises, L. von. *Human Action: A Treatise on Economics*, pp. 244–56 and pp. 479–537.
Rothbard, M. N. *Man, Economy, and State: A Treatise on Economic Principles*, pp. 273–433.

7. FROM AN EVENLY ROTATING ECONOMY TO THE REAL WORLD

In an evenly rotating economy, the problem of resource allocation would be easily solved. Knowledge of future preferences, resources, and techniques of production would be the result of a world without change. Equipped with this knowledge, market participants would be able to devote resources to their most satisfying lines of use without friction and inconsistent planning. Units of factors of production would be priced equal to their discounted marginal value product, thereby permitting investor-producers to earn only an interest return. Units of factors would be repeatedly employed in the same fashion as in the past, since to change particular usages would require the creation of a lower marginal value product, an inferior result that could be anticipated in advance and obviated. The known money values of future products would indicate the money values of resources to be used in their creation.

However, everyone knows that the real world is not a world of mere constants and perfect predictability. There is really no assurance about tomorrow. The tastes and value scales of individuals do not remain constant, and neither can anyone assume that the nature and amount of available resources will remain the same. And with time comes continuous revision in the recipes and techniques of production. Thus in the real world there is no simple and automatic solution to the task of resource allocation. Because of the ever-present factor of uncertainty, no actor "knows" the future; each can only attempt to forecast it in terms of his own understanding of the potentiality of the present.

Nevertheless, the concept of the ERE is useful in explaining and understanding the real world of change. In the midst of continuous change, the market is relentlessly in pursuit of a general equilibrium in which all productive factors are being applied to their most desired uses and all profits and losses have disappeared. In other words, the tendency of the real market is to be always moving toward an evenly rotating economy. It is the factor of change that prevents that economy from ever being reached. With the conditions and data of the market being subject to constant change, revisions and adjustments in plans and actions are continually necessitated.

The concept of an ERE helps one to imagine a world in which changes in tastes, resources, and technology have ceased. More importantly, it yields an understanding of the direction that the market is continually taking as errors emanating from the imperfect knowledge of the future give rise to revised plans and actions on the part of market participants.

For example, when producers underestimate the demand for a particular good, the resulting higher price of the good attracts more resources to that use and away from less important uses. As more attention is given to the production of this good, its unit price falls and the unit price of its resources rises, gradually eliminating the opportunity to profit from its production.

This is a process of adjusting to facts of the market that were not knowable in advance. Through this adjusting process, the market continually strives to reach the state of the ERE; the problem is that this quest is constantly interrupted and sidetracked as a result of subsequent change and its complement, the need for additional adjustment. It should be clear that the imaginary ERE is not being held up as some kind of ideal economy. Its purpose is only to help explain the workings of the real market economy. The contrast between the real world and the ERE is described by Rothbard:

> The difference in the dynamic, real world is this. None of these future values or events is known; all must be estimated, guessed at, by the capitalists. They must advance present money in a speculation upon the unknown future in the expectation that the future product will be sold at a remunerative price. In the real world, then, quality of judgment and accuracy of forecast play an enormous role in the incomes acquired by capitalists. As a result of the arbitrage of the entrepreneurs, the tendency is always toward the ERE; in consequence of ever-changing reality, changes in value scales and resources, the ERE never arrives.[1]

This whole matter of the constant changeability of market conditions is the essence of the concept of uncertainty, as distinguished earlier from the concept of quantifiable risk. The key to this distinction is that the interrelationship of events and factors in the competitive market is so complex that it precludes the precise calculation of probability of the success or failure of any given entrepreneurial decision. Market conditions at any instant are comparatively unique; they do not lend themselves to the gathering of extensive empirical data that can be said to relate to homogeneous circumstances and events. Accurate anticipations of consumer preferences, competitor actions, technological change, and resource availabilities are far more difficult to make than typical actuarial predictions.

Actuarial predictions deal with matters that have an extensive history, are subject to detailed classification, and occurred under conditions that can be expected to remain for the most part unchanged for the time being. Businessmen, however, do not have the fortune of operating under many of these repetitive sequences of highly categorized events. As Knight has

---

[1]Rothbard, *Man, Economy, and State*, p. 464.

said, the problem stems from the inability to accumulate sufficient empirical data relating to particular classes of subjects and events. As Hayek has put it, "In the social sciences we have to deal with. . .phenomena which are not made up of sufficiently large numbers of similar events to enable us to ascertain the probabilities of their occurrence."[2]

All of this is not to say that businessmen have absolutely no sense of what future developments are likely to be. They do make judgments and predictions about the future. But the point is that these anticipations are speculative and not mathematically precise. It is not that there are *no* indications concerning the future; it is that there is grossly incomplete knowledge of future developments. The following statements by Knight are pertinent:

> It is a world of change in which we live, and a world of uncertainty. We live only by knowing *something* about the future; while the problems of life, or of conduct at least, arise from the fact that we know so little. This is as true of business as of other spheres of activity. The essence of the situation is action according to *opinion*, of greater or less foundation and value, neither entire ignorance nor complete and perfect information, but partial knowledge.[3]

Entrepreneurial Profits and Losses

Profit theory has often explained the emergence of money profits in the market economy either as a reward for taking risks or as the natural income earned by capital (as opposed to the rents of land and wages of labor) in the classical sense. Both of these analyses are incorrect. In the competitive market, all business activity is risky in the sense of being uncertain; yet not every business venture is monetarily profitable. A businessman who makes too many mistakes is not automatically rewarded with profits simply because he undertook ventures of a risky nature. Profits cannot be called simply a reward for risk-taking. The classical thesis that profits are the return peculiar to the category of capital or capital goods is an empty explanation because it fails to show just why something extra should arise from the usage of capital and not from the usage of the other factors of land and labor. At times this theory borders on a sort of normal interest theory, but it lacks the principle of time-preference and is mistaken in tying interest only to capital goods. As has been shown, the phenomenon of interest is present in all matters involving the exchange of present goods for future goods.

Profits, which are nonexistent in the evenly rotating economy, are received by those entrepreneur-producers who most correctly anticipate

[2]F. A. Hayek, "Coping with Ignorance," *Imprimis* 7, no. 7, (1978).
[3]Knight, *Risk, Uncertainty, and Profit*, p. 199.

the wishes of the consumers. Profits arise when productive factors are bought for prices lower than the prices for which their products are sold. In a world of uncertainty, the producers have to judge what the marginal value product will be for units of productive factors. Those who are able to discern discrepancies between current resource prices and the future prices of their products generate money revenues in excess of money costs by capitalizing on such opportunities. In such cases the resources can be said to have been underpriced. The ultimate prices of consumer goods are determined by the subjective valuations placed by consumers on the goods offered for sale. Thus the crucial task of the entrepreneur-producer in purchasing various units of resources is to anticipate as correctly as possible the future preferences of consumers. Using such anticipations, he is able to impute an anticipated marginal value product to the available factors of production.

Profits result if others have failed to value the particular factor units as highly and if it turns out that the entrepreneur-producer was reasonably correct in his anticipations. On the other hand, losses result whenever he acquires resources at amounts greater than the money value of the products generated from such resources. In these cases the resources can be said to be overpriced for the purposes to which they were put. Since there is no certainty about the future, there is room in the market economy for entrepreneurial losses as well as profits. Profits, then, do arise in connection with risk-taking but only when the anticipations turn out to be correct.

A theory of profits should also include a corollary explanation of losses. The principal determinant of business success is the foresight and alertness of those in charge of directing the business. Mises has explained the source of money profits in the following way:

> The ultimate source from which entrepreneurial profit and loss are derived is the uncertainty of the future constellation of demand and supply.
>
> If all entrepreneurs were to anticipate correctly the future state of the market, there would be neither profits nor losses. The prices of all the factors of production would already today be fully adjusted to tomorrow's prices of products. In buying the factors of production the entrepreneur would have to expend (with due allowance for the difference between the prices of present goods and future goods) no less an amount than the buyers will pay him later for the product. An entrepreneur can make a profit only if he anticipates future conditions more correctly than other entrepreneurs. Then he buys the complementary factors of production at prices the sum of which, including allowance for the time difference, is smaller than the price at which he sells the product.[4]

---

[4]Mises, *Human Action*, pp. 293–94.

It should be realized that the phenomenon of entrepreneurial profits and losses continues to occur only because there are persistent changes in market conditions. This is what was meant when it was earlier stated that the concept of the evenly rotating economy provides an understanding of the goal toward which the market continuously moves but never reaches. If new changes in market data were not to constantly occur, the prices of all complementary resources would be finally set so that total money costs would equal total money revenues and there would be nothing left for profits and losses. There is an inherent tendency for profits and losses to disappear as entrepreneurs make adjustments in their plans, moving into profitable lines and away from unprofitable ones. It is the recurrence of change and discovery in market conditions that precludes the permanent and complete elimination of profits and losses.

Consumer Valuations and Productive Resources

It has already been shown that the subjective valuations of consumers are the principal determinant in establishing prices of consumer goods. And the vital connection between the prices of consumer goods and the prices of factors of production was demonstrated in describing the conditions of the evenly rotating economy. In the ERE the prices of resources are derived from the money value of the product created. This essential relationship between the prices of final and intermediate goods and services is no less applicable in the dynamic market economy. Just as in the ERE, entrepreneurs bid for units of resources in the real market in light of their expected marginal value product. Prices of consumer goods are not set by simply adding up the money costs of production. The value scales of consumers determine the prices of produced consumer goods, and it is these expected prices of consumer goods that provide the basis for entrepreneurial bidding for units of scarce resources that are utilized in the generation of consumer goods. The process is the same as it would be in the ERE, except that in the real world product value cannot be imputed to the means of production with certainty.

The entrepreneur-producer's failure to see that the prices of productive resources arise from the expected price of his product occurs because he sees his costs as being externally determined and simply given. His problem, as he sees it, is to place available resources in productive uses that will yield revenues sufficiently in excess of these costs. But if the broader view that the economist takes is considered, one realizes that the prices of resources, or costs, stem from widespread bidding by countless participants since most factors can be employed in a wide variety of productive uses. Underlying all of this bidding are the anticipated marginal value products as envisioned by the various producers. For a highly nonspecific factor of production, the unit price that any given producer pays reflects the expected marginal value product of that factor in alternative uses, the culmination of bidding on the part of innumerable and diverse firms. The acceptance of a "given" price by the individual entrepreneur-producer actually contributes another bid to the market process.

The derivation of prices of highly specialized factors from the expected value of their product is even more obvious. The price of this type of resource is actually far more sensitive to changes in the price of its product than is the price of a highly versatile resource to changes in the price of any *particular* product for which it is being used because the economic fate of the versatile factor is not so dependent upon how well any particular product fares economically. The gradations of its value in alternative uses entail much narrower gaps than does a specific resource whose value in some other use by definition approaches zero. One only needs to consider the predicament of the owner of cigarette machines if the demand for cigarettes were to significantly diminish or increase to grasp the relationship between product prices and the prices of specific resources.

The producer who sells his product to other producers rather than the ultimate consumer does not escape the influence of consumer valuations on the price of his product. The producer who purchases his product to be used further in the production process or to be sold to other producers or ultimate consumers will see the product in terms of what he in turn can sell the good or its product for. The influence of consumer valuations is pervasive regardless of the number of stages through which the resources pass before their culmination in the final consumer good. At some final level, producers who sell directly to consumers must directly impute dollar values expressive of consumer preferences to the resources and services purchased. It is this front line of producers who set the imputation of consumer prices to resource prices in motion, and this imputative relationship permeates every prior stage of the production process. No seller of producer goods and services can long stay in a particular line of business if the ultimate consumer good into whose production his product or service enters has grown unpopular, regardless of how many stages or levels removed from the final product his contribution is.

Sellers of producer goods and services may well be able to concern themselves only with the expected prices to be paid by their own customers, and not trouble themselves with the prices that will eventually be paid by consumers. Yet it cannot be ignored long that these immediate prices mirror over time the anticipated final prices, and this fact becomes more apparent the further one moves along the production process toward product completion. The closer to completion the intermediate goods become, the more specific they are and the closer the tie between them and the ultimate consumer good. For example, iron is more convertible than iron tubes, and iron tubes are more convertible than iron machine parts. In a modern economy the advent of intricate capital goods creates a serious issue of convertibility in a market environment of changing conditions. Less advanced times were characterized by far more flexible, though less productive, means of production. Mises has explained this dominant role of the consumers in the economic process of the market economy:

> The consumers determine ultimately not only the prices of the consumers' goods, but no less the prices of all factors of production. They determine the income of every member of the market economy. . . . The competition between the entrepreneurs reflects the prices of consumers' goods in the formation of the factors of production. . . . It makes effective the subsumed decisions of the consumers as to what purpose the non-specific factors should be used for and to what extent the specific factors of production should be used.[5]

Of course, in the midst of the uncertainty and extremely long channels of production that characterize modern market economy, there is plenty of room for error in pricing based on expected consumer preferences and product prices. As noted earlier, those who make too many mistakes are penalized by financial loss, and those who are more correct in their anticipations reap financial profits. Changes in market conditions are particularly harsh for the owners of capital goods that are not easily convertible to other uses. The owner of cigarette machines could be ruined if there were a widespread fall in the demand for cigarettes.

At any given moment capital goods are appraised exclusively from the point of view of their future usefulness. This potential usefulness is not merely a matter of technological usefulness but embraces the monetary significance of the item's anticipated product. Thus a relatively new machine can be rendered obsolete and virtually worthless as a result of changes in market data. The entrepreneur does not appraise his complex of productive factors from the standpoint of how much he expended for them in the past. As Jevons said, "In commerce bygones are forever bygones. . . . Industry is essentially prospective, not retrospective." This is the essential meaning of the concept of "sunk costs." Mises cogently makes the same point: "Errors committed in the past in the production of capital goods available today do not burden the buyer; their incidence falls entirely on the seller. In this sense the entrepreneur who proceeds to buy against money capital goods for future production crosses out the past."[6]

It can then be seen that nonspecific resources like raw iron and labor can be used to produce a specialized machine whose product is no longer

[5]Mises, *Human Action*, p. 271.
[6]Ibid., p. 505.

important to the consuming public. This means that the money value of the machine would bear no relationship to the money costs of the versatile inputs whose usefulness has been dissipated in the conversion process. In retrospect, it would have been better had the versatile resource units been devoted to more desirable conversions. But such mistakes are likely to occur in the absence of perfect knowledge of the future.

The Consequences of the Past

Although all action is oriented to the future, one must not overlook the influence of the past on production. The fact that changes in market conditions render an inconvertible capital good technically inferior to a more modern type does not mean that it is necessarily economically feasible to abandon the inferior good and shift to the superior one. One is certainly justified in saying that in retrospect committing resources to a form that eventually becomes inferior is economically wasteful. The entry of the asset on the owner's books would show this economic loss. It may be, however, that the inferior machine can still be used in competition with the superior one. Whether the inferior machine should remain in use or be abandoned for the more modern one depends on how well the latter performs.

The decision hinges on the net revenues that can be expected from each alternative from the present moment on. The additional cost of implementing the technologically superior machine may be too great to warrant the shift. The inferior machine is already in existence and its original cost is thus no longer relevant. On the other hand, the cost of the superior machine is still relevant because no decision on it has been made and no money has been committed for its acquisition. If the net revenues expected from continued use of the inferior machine are greater than that expected from alternative uses (including scrapping), then this continued use is economical.

The complaint that things would be better if the inferior machine had never been provided serves no purpose now. The task is to make the best of things as they now exist. This is what Mises means when he says, "History and the past have their say."[7]

The influence of the past has the same application to the question of advantageous and disadvantageous locations of inconvertible capital goods. Changes in market conditions can result in a plant's location becoming less desirable than some other place of operation, but costs of relocating can prohibit a shift in spite of the desirability of the new location.

[7]Ludwig V. Mises, *Epistemological Problems of Economics* (Princeton: D. Van Nostrand Co., Inc., 1960), p. 220.

Unrestricted and Restricted Markets

The economic analysis in this book deals primarily with a market economy in which there exist comparatively few artificial restrictions on the economic activities of its members. It is this relatively unhampered market that tends to direct resources so that, as Mises says, "No want more urgently felt should remain unsatisfied because the means suitable for its attainment were employed—wasted—for the attainment of a want less urgently felt." The importance of the subjective valuations of producers and consumers has been emphasized already. The unhampered market recognizes the wants of every individual, regardless of his function as a buyer or seller. (Actually, each able person performs both roles in the market economy.)

The significant point here is that although the wants of the consumers are preeminent regarding the goods and services offered for sale in the market, the ultimate decision to choose between the monetary reward of the market and the advantages of other pursuits is left up to each individual. Employees and investors act on the basis of nonmonetary as well as monetary factors. The sovereignty of the consumers is not unlimited.

It should be clear, however, that artificial restrictions that are granted to some producers and denied to others can be and have been superimposed on the otherwise unhampered market. As a result, restrictions like monopoly rights, patents, and copyrights emerge on the market as economic factors in the same way that other resources gain economic significance. The process of monetary calculation results in the association of economic value with each factor to the extent of its expected contribution to money revenues, which means that market prices can exist for such restrictive factors as transferable franchises, patents, and copyrights. The pricing of such restrictive factors is thus no different from the pricing of resource factors that are not artificially created.[8]

The Social Role of Profits

The objective of entrepreneurial activity in the market economy is to capitalize on opportunities to invest in factors of production at costs that are adequately lower than the revenues subsequently generated by productive activities. Those who are able to achieve this objective successfully receive money profits. The important result of profitable business operations is that resources are thereby diverted away from less desirable

[8]The issue of "monopolistic" restrictions evolving from market forces as opposed to governmental interventions has been widely treated in the economic literature. That these lucrative positions enjoyed by certain market participants can be seen as results of entrepreneurial alertness and anticipation is well argued by Kirzner in his *Competition and Entrepreneurship* (Chicago: University of Chicago Press, 1973).

uses into uses that better suit the wishes of consumers. Profits, then, serve a vital social purpose. In a changing world there is always an opportunity to improve the way things are done. Improvements may take the form of more satisfying products and services or more efficient ways of generating presently preferred products and services.

So long as the ways of doing things are not frozen and people are not barred from pursuing improvements, profits will always occur and be a necessary part of the market economy. Only in the imaginary and static economy of the ERE are all opportunities for improvement in resource utilization exhausted. It is clear that changes in either preferences, resources, or technology call for rearrangements in the employment of available resources.

The emergence of discrepancies between product prices and the prices of the complementary factors of production signals to market participants that adjustments are in order. Profitable discrepancies attract increased assignment of resources to those particular lines of application; this extension is accompanied by higher unit prices of resources used and lower unit prices of those particular products. Over time the price discrepancies are eliminated in those particular lines; profits for those businesses disappear, at least until new discrepancies are discovered or created.

The superior foresight of the successful entrepreneur-producer does not benefit him permanently because others follow his example and lower his profits.[9] If the difference between total money costs and total money revenues goes the opposite way and financial losses instead of profits are the result, adjustments are made in the other direction. Relevant factors of production are reshuffled into other employments until losses in the original lines of business are terminated and profit prospects restored. The occurrence of financial losses shows that resources would be better used elsewhere, that they have been put to uses that are inferior to alternative lines of employment as represented by their prevailing market prices.

It is the ceaseless search on the part of entrepreneurs for profitable opportunities that leads to the allocation of scarce resources to their most desirable productive usages. Along the way, they wipe out the discrepancies between resource values and product values and thereby remove market inconsistencies. Discrepancies between factor and product money values simultaneously expose existing misallocations of resources and promote corrective action in providing profit opportunities. It is thus important to realize, as Kirzner has pointed out, that "the entrepreneurial

---

[9]This statement is true except for the rare and unlikely situation of complete ownership of a critical resource by a single entrepreneur-producer who is thereby insulated from competition from others. See Kirzner, *Competition and Entrepreneurship*. Both the total ownership by one owner and the nonsubstitutability of other resources required in this situation are extremely unlikely occurrences.

62

search for profits implies a *search for situations where resources are mis-allocated.*[10] The crucial role of the entrepreneur, hence of profits, in the market economy is of utmost significance.

> For it is impossible to eliminate the entrepreneur from the picture of the market economy. The various complementary factors of production cannot come together spontaneously. They need to be combined by the purposive efforts of men aiming at certain ends and motivated by the urge to improve their state of satisfaction. In eliminating the entrepreneur one eliminates the driving force of the whole market system.[11]

Although there would be neither entrepreneurs nor entrepreneurial profits in an ERE, it has been shown that there would exist an interest income for the producers who invest present money for future money. In the real world of change and profits, the time-preference principle is no less operative. This means that conceptually there can be recognized the phenomenon of interest in the market economy. However, because of the factor of uncertainty, each investment of present money is faced with the possibility of failure and loss. Consequently, the so-called rate of interest actually constitutes a combination of time and uncertainty factors that are intertwined to give a single rate. The distinction can be made only conceptually as the factor of uncertainty surrounds every instance of investment. The perception of varying degrees of uncertainty accounts for the structure of varying so-called rates of interest.

At the outset of this overview of the Austrian analysis of the market economy, it was stressed that in an economy of exchange, advanced and developed through specialization and the division of labor, two absolutely essential requirements must be satisfied. The first was the need for a common basis for calculating the relative merits of alternative resource employments. Calculations in kind were seen to be insufficient for the rational allocation of scarce resources in an advanced economy. This requirement calls for some medium through which the preferences of the members of the society, its consumers, could be expressed to and discerned by the employers of the productive resources. The second was the need for a means by which the decisions and actions of scattered and separate actors can be coordinated. It was concluded that both of these requirements are met by the use of a common means of exchange and its counterpart, money prices. Economic calculation, predicated upon a system of market prices, emerges as the indispensable means of effective resource employment.

It can now be seen that through the economic calculations of entre-

[10]I. M. Kirzner, *Market Theory and the Price System* (Princeton: D. Van Nostrand Co., Inc., 1963), p. 303.
[11]Mises, *Human Action*, pp. 248, 249.

preneur-producers, there is a rational process of factor utilization. These calculations are developed with the guidance of past market prices and money results and through projected market prices and monetary results relating to various resources and final products. The advent of change in market conditions is reflected in certain price changes that signal for different courses of action to be taken to enhance the effectiveness of resource employment. Without the system of money prices and the ability to calculate expected results of various actions in terms that afford comparisons, there would be no way rationally to plan production activities on a scale characteristic of an advanced economy.

Efficient resource utilization necessitates some means by which prospective alternative lines of use can be related as well as possible to each prospective result or product. Although it is tenuous and imprecise, monetary calculation provides this means. And although erroneous calculations can be made because of poor judgment, resulting in the misallocation of resources, they can be quickly rectified by the financial loss revealed in retrospective calculation.

It bears repeating that monetary calculation is not concerned with the measurement of value. The task of resource allocation can be accomplished if calculations afford guidance to the relative importance of various uses and products. Monetary profits and losses indicate the more desirable and the less desirable applications of units of scarce resources. Although it is prospective monetary calculation that is primary, retrospective calculations of profit and loss are important both instructionally and in guiding decisions about capital maintenance and capital consumption. The concepts of capital and income, profit and loss, revenues and costs, provide the rational basis for resource allocations in the market economy. The allocation process is thereby purposive and not haphazard.

Suggested Readings

Kirzner, I. M. *Competition and Entrepreneurship.* Chicago: University of Chicago Press, 1973.

———. *Market Theory and the Price System,* pp. 297–309.

Mises, L. von. *Human Action: A Treatise on Economics,* pp. 289–326.

Rothbard, M. N. *Man, Economy, and State: A Treatise on Economic Principles,* pp. 463–559.

8. INFLATION AND THE BUSINESS TRADE CYCLE

Thus far all explanation of the market system has been predicated on the assumption that there is no inflation problem and no erratic business pattern of intermittent general expansion followed by general recession or depression. The market system has been shown to operate through the price mechanism, which induces adaptive and complementary actions on the part of market participants in the face of ever-changing market conditions. There is nothing inherent in this system to produce a general or widespread increase in prices or to lead to pervasive business expansion and then general business contraction. Changes in specific prices, i.e., relative price changes, abound, mirroring changes in valuations and available supplies. These price shifts include increases and decreases; absent is any factor to cause most prices to increase over time. Characteristic too are errors on the part of some entrepreneur-producers who suffer money losses from malinvestments. Yet there is no causal element that leads to widespread malinvestment and the attendant general recession or depression. That these occurrences of a general rise in prices and the ebb and flow of general business activity pertain to our world today hardly needs mentioning. What is of significance to us here is their cause.

Popular use of the term *inflation* to mean a general rise in prices misconstrues the fundamental problem by focusing on the effect and not the cause. It is the inflation of the money supply by the U. S. Treasury and the central banking system that engenders in the structure of market prices a general upward movement over time. The printing of additional Federal Reserve notes and the creation of new demand deposits in connection with the monetization of federal debt along with fractional-reserve banking and member-bank borrowing (discounting) from Federal Reserve banks constitute the basic mechanisms of inflation of the money supply. These are all forms of credit expansion, which means the injection of additional money into the system. A continuous rise in prices in general is the natural outcome of a continuous policy of credit expansion.

We have seen already that the interest rate reflects the ratio of present goods valuation to future goods valuation. If there is a shift toward a greater preference of present goods over future goods, then the interest rate increases correspondingly, reflecting the greater discount of future goods. Conversely, a change in favor of more future goods would lead to a lowering of the interest rate. The market interest rate tends toward a level at which the amount of funds that savers are willing to invest in produc-

tion equals the amount that entrepreneur-producers are willing to obtain
and use for productive purposes.

The saving-investment of funds means that purchasing power is used so
that a certain amount of resources is directed toward the production of
capital goods as opposed to consumer goods. As we have seen, capital
goods production generally lengthens the production process, i.e., roundabout production is expanded. However, capital goods production might
also require a lateral expansion of production in the form of additional
plants and equipment similar to existing ones. It is important to stress that
the market rate of interest provides a signal that indicates the extent to
which capital goods production may be undertaken without frustrating
the demand for consumer goods. The savings made available for business
investment at the market interest rate are thereby intentionally withdrawn by the savers from the otherwise potential demand for consumer
goods. Entrepreneur-producers are being allowed to use these funds to
employ resources in the productive process in view of whatever profit opportunities they perceive and choose to pursue. And yet these production
decisions are not without restraint:

> The role which the rate of interest plays in these deliberations of the
> planning businessman is obvious. It shows him how far he can go in
> withholding factors of production from employment for want-
> satisfaction in nearer periods of the future and in dedicating them to
> want-satisfaction in remoter periods. It shows him what period of
> production conforms in every concrete case to the difference which
> the public makes in the ratio of valuation between present goods and
> future goods. It prevents him from embarking upon projects the exe-
> cution of which would not agree with the limited amount of capital
> goods provided by the saving public.[1]

The expansion of credit, i.e., the increase in the money supply, through
the joint action of the federal government and the banking system tends to
lower the interest rate below a level that would otherwise prevail in a
market devoid of such actions to increase the money supply. In the early
stages of the credit expansion the interest rate actually drops. Subsequently, as the effect of such policies on prices throughout the market becomes
apparent, a price premium is added to the interest rate in order to protect
the savers from the harmful impact of expected price increases. Note,
however, that this price premium starts *after* the price effects have occurred so that, in largely mirroring such effects, it must necessarily lag
behind what would be adequate to cover further price increases under
continuing inflation. Because of the price premium, the interest rate tends
to rise over time despite continued additions to the money supply. Never-

[1]Mises, *Human Action*, p. 547.

theless, continued doses of additional money dampens this rise in the interest rate so that it "continues to lag behind the height at which it would cover both ordinary interest plus the positive price premium."[2]

The fact that interest rates reach levels uncharacteristic of years past does not invalidate the point that the rates are kept artificially lower than rates adequate to cover the discount, entrepreneurial, and inflation elements. The often heard complaint that interest rates are too high under these conditions is a misconception. We have just seen that there are two factors that tend to hold down the rate of interest below the level sufficient to allow for the related elements emerging on the market: (1) The implementation of the price premium lags behind the changes in purchasing power stemming from the inflation; and (2) the additional supply of money thrown onto the market has a dampening effect on the interest rate. Concerning the latter point, it must be realized that entrepreneur-producers are unable to differentiate between additional funds that have been artificially created and additional funds emanating from real savings.

Decreased interest rates in the early stages of the credit expansion emerge as faulty signals to entrepreneur-producers about the real savings available for business investment purposes. Business decisions are made as if the ratio of present (consumer) goods to future (capital) goods had dropped, when in actuality no such change has occurred. Additional investments in capital goods, broadening and lengthening the structure of production, are spurred as a business boom gets underway. Resources are diverted into the production of capital goods, and the prices of such resources are concomitantly bid up in the process. Yet the cue that the entrepreneur-producers have followed, the interest rate, has been falsified by the effects of the credit expansion. From the viewpoint of the general public it would be better that such resources not be misdirected in this fashion. Real savings appropriately available for additional capital goods formation has not increased.

Under the conditions of a short-lived credit expansion, the boom can be only temporary. The demand for consumer goods has not dropped, and the impropriety of enlarging and lengthening the production process as if it had is revealed once the credit expansion is terminated. The costs invested are seen as unjustified because the longer waiting time to complete and implement the additional capacity to produce is inappropriate in view of the unaffected demand for consumer goods. Production expansions cannot be finished, and the structure of production, which involves the coordination of numerous links in the lengthened production chain, is thrown out of smooth running order. Liquidations and rearrangements of

[2]Ibid., p. 552.

production are necessary in order to correct the undesirable and unforeseen effects of the malinvestments. The actual consumption-saving ratio is once again able to dictate the balance between shorter and longer or more roundabout approaches to production. The correction or adjustment process is what is commonly referred to as a recession or depression.

If the duration of the credit expansion is not short, then the extent of malinvestments is compounded and the inevitable and eventual correction process is intensified. The continuous flow of additional credit enables the illusion to persist of greater savings as indicated by dampened interest rates in the midst of booming business. The additional purchasing power entering the market through the capital goods industries leads to increases in the demand for and prices of consumer goods. It appears to the entrepreneur-producers that the higher costs involved in continuing the capital goods expansion will be justified. The error in their expectations is hidden by the effects of the steady stream of additional credit. The additional credit accommodates their need for more funds to carry out the completion of their ventures in the face of rising costs. The boom must stop once the credit expansion is terminated. At that time, the correction process, i.e., a recession or depression, is ushered in.

The decision not to halt the credit expansion eventually must lead to what Mises has called the "crack-up boom," characterized by a general flight into real values and the collapse of the monetary system. In the later stages of the expansion the additions to the money supply must be increasingly accelerated as market participants have come to expect ever-increasing prices. At some point, the system of monetary exchange must break down. Consequently, to continue the easy-money policy in order to avoid the otherwise inevitable depression must bring about an even harsher fate: the collapse of the monetary system and the market economy, with its great advantages of specialization and division of labor.

The evidence of recent years indicates that it is unlikely that the credit expansion will be so protracted and uninterrupted that a crack-up boom will occur. It appears that, as dictated by political exigencies, intermittent expansion and contraction of the money supply generating a cyclical process that "becomes self-perpetuating and proceeds to the 'stop-go cycle'"[3] is the pattern likely to prevail. This means that with shorter-lived expansions the corrections or adjustments are less severe, and thus emerges the familiar and softer term "recession" in lieu of "depression."

It is important to see that the intervening in the market by increasing the money supply sidetracks the market process from its natural tendency

[3]Gerald P. O'Driscoll, Jr., *Economics as a Coordination Problem* (Kansas City: Sheed, Andrews, and McMeel, Inc.), p. 114.

But without this false credit would the system survive?

inflation creates depression.

68   to coordinate the actions of various market participants. The problem of inflation, then, is not merely a problem of a deteriorating monetary unit. The title and essence of O'Driscoll's book appropriately asserts the pre-eminence of the problem of coordination, especially when exacerbated by inflation. The problem with inflation is that it cuts at the heart of the market process, producing at best intermittent and disruptive cyclical swings and at worst the disastrous cessation of market exchange as it is known in highly industrialized societies.

Suggested Readings

Hayek, F. A. *Monetary Theory and the Trade Cycle.* Clifton, N.J.: Kelly, 1975.

Mises, L. von. *Human Action: A Treatise on Economics*, pp. 538–586.

O'Driscoll, G. P., Jr. *Economics as a Coordination Problem: The Contributions of Friedrich A. Hayek.* Kansas City: Sheed, Andrews, and McMeel, Inc., 1977.

Adam Smith Institute

Purpose of the Institute

The Adam Smith Institute is an independent, nonpartisan, educational foundation, operating in both Britain and the United States. Supporting and disseminating scholarly research into policy choice, the institute is especially concerned with the introduction of innovative proposals and creative thought into the area of public policy debate.

The institute's programme of research studies, publications, seminars and information services enables it to promote the study of ideas which have been successfully applied in other countries, and to develop original policy options. The institute is able, through its programme, to study and communicate ideas to people at every level of public policy debate.

Academic Advisory Board

The work of the institute is assisted by an academic advisory board of the following members:

Chairman: Professor F. A. Hayek. Members: Professor Stanislav Andreski, Dr. Eamonn Butler, Dr. Stuart Butler, Professor Brian Cox, Professor Antony Flew, Professor Cyril Grunfeld, Dr. Madsen Pirie, Mr. Victor Serebriakoff, Mr. T. E. Utley, Professor Ernest van den Haag, Professor Esmond Wright.

The Carl Menger Society

The Carl Menger Society is an independent society of economists and other individuals, dedicated to the study and promulgation of the principles of the Austrian school of economics. It takes its name from the founder of the Austrian tradition, Carl Menger, whose intellectual successors include Ludwig von Mises, Israel Kirzner, Ludwig Lachmann and F. A. Hayek.

The society holds regular conferences on key issues in Austrian economics.